ADVENTURES OF MS KELLY IN MIAMI

BY

CALVIN DIRICKSON

Order this book online at www.trafford.com
or email orders@trafford.com

Most Trafford titles are also available at major online book retailers.

Note for Librarians: A cataloguing record for this book is available from Library
and Archives Canada at www.collectionscanada.ca/amicus/index-e.html

Printed in Victoria, BC, Canada.

ISBN: 978-1-4269-1038-8 (Soft)
ISBN: 978-1-4269-1040-1 (e-book)

*We at Trafford believe that it is the responsibility of us all, as both individuals
and corporations, to make choices that are environmentally and socially sound.
You, in turn, are supporting this responsible conduct each time you purchase a
Trafford book, or make use of our publishing services. To find out how you are
helping, please visit www.trafford.com/responsiblepublishing.html*

*Our mission is to efficiently provide the world's finest, most comprehensive
book publishing service, enabling every author to experience success.
To find out how to publish your book, your way, and have it available
worldwide, visit us online at www.trafford.com*

Trafford rev. 10/12/2009

 www.trafford.com

North America & international
toll-free: 1 888 232 4444 (USA & Canada)
phone: 250 383 6864 ♦ fax: 812 355 4082 ♦ email: info@trafford.com

ACKNOWLEDGEMENTS

To: William Greenfield for all his help
in editing and illustrating.

To: My wonderful children Kathryn Ann
Dirickson and Douglas Andrew Dirickson.

To: My sister-in-law Mary Ann Wright for her
continued support of me and my children.

To: My wonderful neighbor Patricia
Difurio who loves Ms Kelly dearly

To: All animal lovers and the animal protection
originations through out the world.

FORWARD

I hope you enjoy this my second book of my many Adventures. Let me give you a word of advice. If you haven't read my first book "Adventures of Ms Kelly in Tallahassee by all means get you a copy and read it first. Several times I refer back to my days on the little farm in Tallahassee in this book. You will enjoy my books much more by reading them in order.

My master, Calvin Dirickson and I are busy writing my third book. "Adventures of Ms Kelly in Nevada"

Actually these three books are the story of my life. I do all the talking in my books. My master just puts everything down on paper for me. A real cute guy name Bill helped in illustrating my books and painted my picture.

My books are not only for the young but for animal lovers of all ages, especially animal lovers that have or have had a dog for a pet.

Calvin and I have our own language. You can learn how to communicate with your pet by reading my books.

Check out my books and my master's autobiography at www. mskelly-purplerobin.com
Please support your local animal shelter
Thank you

ONE

THE LAKE MONSTER

I'm very sad as I bid my Mother and Father good-by. I'm quite sure that I will never see them again. With tears in my eyes I keep looking back until the puppy mill is out of sight.

I slowly turned and look at Calvin then out the windshield at the road ahead. We have a long journey to our new home and life in Miami Florida.

I'm seeing new things almost every mile that we traveled. The landscape is much different than Tallahassee's. Here it's all flat land and in some places underwater.

I'm so excited I can't sit still. I know Calvin is getting tired of me running back and forth across the front seat. I have to run to his side of the van, jump up in his lap and watch everything out of his window. Then I see something interesting from the other side and have to run back to that side to see what is going on there. I want to see everything but can't watch out both sides at the same time.

"Ms Kelly will you settle down, you can't see everything." Calvin said in an irritated voice. I settled down and just sat on my pillow, in the middle of the front seat and took in all I could see from my bed.

All the trees down here are, Palms, Oranges or Grapefruits, and the land is flat, not a lot to look at. In Tallahassee there are hills and many different kind of trees, I'm already missing our home on the old dirt lane.

I heard Calvin on his cell phone telling a friend that we just went through Orlando. He said, "Only two hundred more miles, Ms Kelly is about to wear me down."

We stopped at a building that is in the middle of the four lane highway. I heard someone call it a rest area. Calvin took me out for a walk so I could potty. I don't know how he knew that I needed to go. I was getting desperate to potty.

We are out in the country again; I love the wide open country. I'm a country loving girl. We just passed a heard of cattle and a horse farm. Animal farms are my favorite kind of country, I wish Calvin would stop and settle down here.

I'm getting sleepy; it's time for a nap.

Calvin came to a sudden stop and I woke up. We have stopped to pay a toll. This southern part of Florida cost money just to drive on their roads.

We are now down deep in south Florida and back in a continuing city. I get tired looking out the windows; it's just one house on top of another, so many people and no place for pets to play.

I drifted off to sleep again and when I woke up we are entering a place called Jade Winds. Calvin bought a share in a condo in it. We own half of it and Adrian and his daughter own the other half.

Adrian and Calvin are double cousins and were raised together. They had lost contact with each other years ago. They accidentally met on line in a chat room. During their online chats Adrian told Calvin, "Miami is a good place to retire."

Adrian is dark skinned with a graying beard, I over heard a lady tell him he looks just like Shone Conley. He is very hairy and everybody thinks he is handsome, including me.

I fell in love with Adrian the first day. He complemented me the first time he set eyes on me, by saying, "Ms Kelly you are the cutest dog in the whole universe. You are the most beautiful dog creature I have ever seen!"

His daughter Pam is a nice, dark blond, good looking sixteen year old high school sophomore.

Our condo is on the first floor. It has three bedroom, two bathrooms, kitchen, living and dining room combination. There are two large screened in patios, one is attached to the kitchen and it leads out to an ungodly huge lake.

Calvin and I walked out to the lake. It's so big I can't see across it. Calvin picked me up then I can just barley see houses on the other side of the lake. They looked so small at first I thought they were toy houses.

Calvin and I fell into a routine; we get up early, Calvin fixed coffee and my breakfast. After breakfast we go out to the lake so I can potty.

I love to run up and down the lake shore making the ducks fly and gaze out across the lake. There are hundreds of ducks on the lake and in our condo association and in other condo associations that surround the lake.

There are all kind of tame ducks and one breed of wild ones called Green Heads. It will take me sometime to learn their language. I have never been around ducks.

I ran into a wise old duck, named John Paul, everybody calls him JP for short. He knows some of my language and he volunteered to teach me his. JP told me his language was a lot like that of geese. Since I know the language of geese fluently, I know that I will have no problems learning the duck's language.

There are a lot of cats in the complex. So far I have not run into any that are as mean as Lin and Kim. There are some that don't want anything to do with dogs. They just ignore us instead of wanting to fight.

There are just a few dogs that play outside most just come out to potty. Only small dogs are allowed to live in Jade Winds, even though there are a lot of large ones in the complex. The ones that weigh more than ten pounds are here illegally and their masters only let them out to potty then take them right back in so they will not be discovered and cause trouble between their owners and Jade Winds Condo Association.

Since my hair continues to grown it has to be cut. In the past Calvin clipped my hair but here I was introduced to my first dog salon. The owners and operators are a lady named Donna and her mother Jane, they have a mother and daughter dog grooming salon. This being my first city hair cut I didn't know what to expect and was a little nervous since Calvin had just left me there.

It turned out to be a nice experience; I got a shampoo and haircut and felt great. Jane and Donna treated me like a queen.

It wasn't long after they were through with me that Calvin and Adrian showed up to collect me.

Adrian kept bragging on how great I looked. I pranced around and enjoyed all the great comments about my new hair style.

I overheard Calvin and Donna discussing my schedule, I was to come back every two weeks, the first two visits will be for a shampoo and trim the third appointment will be for a haircut and shampoo. This is great I have my own hair stylist and regular appointments

What a wonderful life I am having. If only my mean brothers could see me now. I know they would be jealous of my success and the great life I am living.

When we got home I scratched on the back door to go out, I didn't have to potty I just wanted to go out and show all the dogs, cats and ducks my new hair style.

I got to know a few of the ducks and was able to talk to them. There are many different kind and colors of tame ducks; the wild ducks, Green Heads are here only in the summer, most of them raise babies during there stay. They all admired my new hair cut. I couldn't help it I had to prance around and show out.

A few days later an old and very wise male duck named Sam said to me, "Ms. Kelly I have heard there is a monster in the lake that loves to eat dogs, especially small ones.

Sam's grandson, Jim, spoke up and said, "Oh Granddad that is just an old mother duck's tale, there is no such thing as a Lake Monster!"

Sam spoke up and said, "Son I have heard that from three different reliable ducks. I honestly believe there is something in that lake that is dangerous. I know there are monsters in the ocean and there is plenty of room in this lake for them."

One early spring day Sam asked me if I would help him out. He said, "There are wild animals called raccoons that come on the property at night and steal duck eggs. The raccoons are afraid of dogs, Ms Kelly can you help us out?"

"Sure, just come to the back door and quack and I will try and get Calvin to let me out, I will be glad to help all I can. I know what a raccoon is; we had a lot of them back in Tallahassee. I also know how do deal with them, normally they are afraid of dogs, if they are not afraid of me because I am so small I will nip them on the rump and then they will be afraid." I explained to Sam.

A couple weeks later, Calvin and I are out by the lake enjoying the early spring warm weather. Della a mother duck came walking by with her brood of eighteen babies. I heard Calvin say to a neighbor, "I have never seen a duck with that many ducklings."

Calvin noticed that one was limping bad and couldn't keep up. He picked the baby duck up and took him in the house. I tried to talk to him but he was so young I could only understand a few words. Calvin bandaged his leg up and fixed him a nest in an empty shoe box. I stayed by the duckling's nest and Calvin put my pillow down beside it so I could guard him at night. I sat for hours watching the duckling sleep. This was making me really want babies of my own.

The next day, the duckling was much better and was able to let me know that he wanted to play with me. Calvin fixed a small pen so he could walk around for exercise. It was big enough for me to get in and the next thing I knew the duckling was asleep laying against me. It felt good to lay with the little duckling.

The more that I am with the duckling, the more I want my own babies.

We kept the duckling in the house for over a week and his leg healed-up well; he could walk and run without limping.

Calvin took him out to the lake and looked for his mother. I didn't know if he would still know who his mother was. I kept saying to him, "We are taking you back to your mommy."

I could recognize her easy, because she is the only mother with eighteen ducklings. The mother duck came out of the lake with her brood. Calvin sat the duckling down in the grass close to the mother. There were a couple quacks between them and mother and baby rushed at each other. She was checking her baby all over making sure he was OK and the duckling was jumping up and flapping its tiny wings for joy. It was a nice reunion.

Sam dropped by during all the commotion and thanked me for taking care of the duckling during the healing of his leg.

Calvin became good friends with a lady name Linda who lived on the third floor of our building.

Linda has three house cats that are very nice.

We go up to see Linda most everyday and I got to know the cats. Jim is an old male cat over ten years old. Tim is also old he is eight, Tammy is the only girl cat and she is three the same age as me.

I loved to go up and play with them they have tons of toys and they would let me play with all of them. They are strictly house cats; Linda would not let them outside.

One day Jim was able to get outside when a neighbor had come in to see Linda and had accidentally left the door open a crack. That was before Calvin and I moved to Jade Winds, JP told me the story. He said, "It became a very bad situation, Jim had walked around the building and got lost. Linda was very upset when no one could find her precious Jim. After the third day and he had not been found the ambulance had to take Linda to the hospital, she had a nervous breakdown. Linda lives alone and her cats are all she has in life. After two weeks they finally found Jim. He was nearly starved to death and had been scared up from fighting with young tomcats."

Jim told JP. "I will never go outside again, I am too old and it is too dangerous."

JP added. "After the ordeal that Jim went through when he got lost outside, Tim and Tammy said that they would never go outside either. All three of them loved to sit in the window and look out at the world."

When we go up to visit Linda and her cats there are two flights of stairs we have to climb, since dogs are not allowed in the elevators. It wasn't long until I knew which door was Linda's and I would run up the stairs and be patiently waiting at Linda's door for Calvin to get to the third floor. Everyone living on the third floor thought I was so smart because I knew where we were going as soon as Calvin started up the stairs.

Calvin took a trip so I was to stay with Donna my hair stylist. Her husband Bill was an animal lover so I got to sleep in bed with them. They have a small dog named Ben. We get along great and have the run of their house at all times. There is a doggie door out to the backyard so we can go out anytime we want to. This is great I was afraid I would be stuck in a cage when Calvin travels out of town.

Calvin took many trips so I got to stay at Donna and Bill's a lot.

One holiday, Calvin and Adrian was taking a trip. Donna and Bill were out of town. Calvin took me to a large vet office that also groomed and boarded dogs.

It was horrible I had to stay in a cage all the time. I was supposed to be taken outside in a doggie run during the day. The place was short of help so they left me in the cage all the time. I was scheduled to get a shot for kennel cough the first day and a bath and shampoo the day that Calvin was to return. I was left in a cage and didn't get anything.

When Calvin came to get me he was extremely mad. I was sick and dirty from not having a bath. The only thing he knew was that I did not get a bath or shampoo. I know if I could just tell him all the other things that they were suppose to do and didn't he would really be mad.

When we got home I was still coughing and by the next morning I was really sick. Calvin took me to a different vet and they told Calvin that I had Kennel Cough. I had to take a painful shot and was sick for a week.

I heard Calvin on the phone and he stopped payment on his credit card for the boarding. He figured out what the cost would be without the shampoo and shots and that was the only amount he would allow his credit company to pay. I was pleased with Calvin's action. I know I will never have to go there again.

The next day I was out late in the evening. I saw a raccoon digging in the grass. I was sure he was looking for duck eggs. I hurried over to where he was. "Mr. Raccoon, get out of here! I will not tolerate you in Jade Winds." I order.

"Little white dog you're a little small to be ordering me around. You mess with me and I'll put a hurting on you."

I was lucky about that time Jerry and Ron a couple beagles came around the building. One of them hollered to me, "Ms Kelly do you need help."

"Mr. Raccoon I have back up so I will tell you once more, you are not allowed in Jade Winds."

"Ok! Since I am out numbered I will go. But you can't watch all day and all night, I will be back and get all the duck eggs I can eat." He threatened.

"I'll be on guard." I replied as I watched him waddle off.

Sam saw all the action and came up after the raccoon was gone and thanked me for running him off.

I was still watching Mr. Raccoon from a distance and he was getting awful close to Sally, a young duck's hidden nest.

"Keep moving Mr. Raccoon I am still watching you!" I ordered.

Every morning after breakfast Calvin would take me out by the lake. It was fun to run along the lakeshore. There are always ducks to play with. They liked for me to chase them and they would pick up and fly over my head and play bomber and dive bomb at me. This is almost as fun as living on the old dirt lane outside of Tallahassee.

One nice warm sunny day, I was walking along close to the water's edge when suddenly————Calvin came running toward me at full speed and was hollering in a loud scary voice, "Ms Kelly get away from the lake!" I couldn't understand why he wanted me away from the water's edge. Then I looked into the water. I could see a huge animal just under the surface. It moved fast and all at once he is in my face! He opened his huge mouth and came at me. He was on me and I froze. I was sure I was a goner. Calvin came running up and kicked the monster in the head just before he clamped down on me with his huge mouth that is full of sharp wicked looking teeth.

The monster turned and came at me again, I ran as fast as I could up the bank but his teeth caught my tail as his mouth clamped shut. He was holding me by the tail and started dragging me backward toward the lake.

I'm in a lot of pain but have to keep my head clear and try to get loose. Calvin was kicking him and I turned and was trying to bite him. He kept slinging me from side to side. I twisted around and as he slung me around I came close to one of his eyes. The next time he slung me around I was ready and bit down as hard and as deep as I could into his eyeball.

He slung me around hard when the pain hit him from his injured eye. His eye was put out and he couldn't see anything on

9

that side. I was trying to dig my front paws in his other eye, trying my best to blind him. I was getting close with my paws to his one good eye. The next time he slung me around I scratched with both of my front paws, as hard and fast as I could at his eyeball. One of my paws got to his good eye and I was able to scratch his eye lid. That did the trick he turned me loose and headed back to the lake with Calvin kicking him and beating him with a broken limb until he got into the lake and went underwater. I bet he will never try to attack us again.

My tail was hurting awful; his teeth had cut through to the bone.

Calvin grabbed me up and headed for the vet's office. I had to take a couple shots and the doctor fitted my tail with a cast.

After we got back to the condo, Calvin said as he held me close, "I can't believe it Ms Kelly you whipped that alligator single handed. What a smart and brave little girl you are."

So that is what the monster is called, an alligator, the old granddaddy duck was correct. There is a monster in the lake.

When we returned I went out the back of the condo, all the cats, dogs, ducks and a couple wild geese had seen the fight. Everyone was trying to talk to me as the same time. All I could hear was, "I can't believe you whipped that monster, how did you do it? You are the bravest and smartest dog I have ever seen."

"I was very lucky to have been able to take the alligator's eye out and get away. I wasn't as brave as everybody thinks. It was pure luck when I was able to twist around and get to his eyes. I will always stay on the top of the bank; never will I go down close to the water line." I explained to the crowd.

I now have the respect from all the animals in Jade Winds. They think I am a brave hero.

I overheard Calvin talking to the President of the Home Owners Association, he said, "There is a six foot alligator in the lake. You need to let all the residents know, I am going to call Animal Control and get someone out here to remove it."

The next day there were several people and animals on the lake bank watching the trapper looking for the alligator. This was a big lake and it would take him a long time to find and trap him.

Calvin told the trapper, "The alligator should be easy to identify since Ms Kelly put out one of his eyes."

The trapper said, "You mean that little dog put the gator's eye out. How in the world did she do it?"

Calvin explained, "The gator was trying to drag her in the water and Ms Kelly turned on him and bit into one of his eyeballs."

It took the trapper a week to catch the alligator. All the animals were sitting on the bank watching as he loaded him up and took him away. He took the alligator to a reptile sanctuary. Since he only had one eye he couldn't survive in the wild anymore. He would have a good home at the sanctuary for the rest of his life.

I heard Calvin telling some of the pet owners, "You must still keep your pets away from the lake. Where there is one gator there is bound to be more. It is easy for them to get in the lake from the swamps.

An Apricot Toy Poodle, named Mike came up to me and was telling me how brave I was to fight off the monster.

I said to him, "That is not a monster it's an alligator and don't you go near the water they love to eat dogs, especially cute ones like you.

Mike looked at me and grinned over my comment about his looks.

I overheard Calvin talking to the President of the Home Owners Association. He was telling him about the same thing that he had said to the pet owners, he repeated, "Even though this gator has been trapped, the security guards must keep an eye out for more, it is easy for them to get into the lake. You must send out letters to all residents about the danger from other alligators.

The lake is dangerous for people and animals; no one should go near the water."

The next morning when Calvin took me out to potty Mike showed up. He asked me if I wanted to play for awhile. I said, "As long as Calvin will let me stay out." We started running and playing and Calvin sat down on a large rock and watching us. He was laughing at us while we ran and played.

Mike told me that he had been rejected as a show dog. I thought he was beautiful and couldn't understand anyone rejecting him. I could tell it bothered him because he didn't make the grade as a show dog. I didn't tell him that I could not even try out for the show business because of my spotted color.

Every morning when Calvin and I went out for our morning walk Mike would show up and join us. I liked Mike he thought I was beautiful; he even complimented me on my spots. I think I am falling for this guy.

After Calvin was sure that I knew what an alligator was and how dangerous it was to go near the lake, he made me a doggie door. Since he was retired most of the time he was home all day anyway.

Where the alligator had bitten my tail, the hair came back in an apricot color. I am glad that those two mean cats, Lin and Kim are not here to tease me about my spotted tail. Mike commented that the spots were beauty marks. This guy has me wrapped around his paw.

Since I have my doggie door I can go outside anytime I want too. Mike and I are always together.

Jade Winds is huge and it has several small ponds through out the complex. This is where most of the ducks stay; those ponds are too small for alligators to hide in.

Mike took me to his house and I met his master, John and his wife, Dorothy. There is also a cat name Blue Boy. I enjoyed going there and John and Dorothy are very nice.

A few months after we had moved to Jade winds, John, Dorothy and Mike knocked on Calvin's door. They came in and introduced themselves, they made small talk for a while and finally came to the reason they came. John said, "Ms Kelly has been coming over and visiting our dog Mike." Mike jumped in John's lap John said pointing to Mike, "This is our dog Mike; he's a registered Apricot Toy Poodle, the same as Ms. Kelly. I would like to propose that Ms Kelly and Mike get married. We would like for them to have a litter of puppies or maybe two litters."

Calvin was speechless; he just stared at Mike and me. I was hoping he would say yes, I wanted some babies of my own.

Finally Calvin said, "I thought about raising show dogs once upon a time, but dismissed the idea as being too much work and time consuming. I wouldn't mind having a couple of Ms Kelly's puppies."

I jumped in his lap and tried to lick his face. He said, "I think Ms Kelly likes the idea too."

Calvin was still a little hesitant and said, ""Lets not get in any hurry; I will have to think this over for a while."

Two

The Mutt Race

Early one warm fall morning Calvin was out back of our condo measuring and driving stakes. It looks like I will be entered into another Mutt race.

I watched, with excitement, as he built my training area. I loved to run and did it every time I was outside. Running back and forth along the lakeshore was one of the fun things that I would do when Calvin took me out to potty.

When I told Mike what Calvin was making, he said, "I have never heard of a Mutt race, what it is?" He had to know all the fine details about the race.

"Its dog races for every breed and every size except greyhounds. It's for pets and they don't have to be registered and can be of mixed breed. It's held once a month in some places and yearly in others. People can put wagers down on them just like they do in the Greyhound races. There is usually a trophy and a large sum of money for the winner. It's loads of fun and I love to participate in the races. When I lived in Tallahassee I could outrun Red and Suzie two of my best friends and both of them were three times my size. Calvin noticed how fast I could run and he entered me in a Mutt race in Monticello, Florida, a small town about twenty miles from Tallahassee and I won." I explained.

After Mike understood everything about the race he became enthused about it. He thought it was great that I had won the Monticello race. He wanted to know if he could enter the next year races. I didn't comment but I knew he was much too slow to participate in the Mutt races. I was afraid he would come in last and be embarrassed.

I began my training early the next morning. Mike volunteered to help. Calvin had driven two stakes down about fifty feet apart. He brought out his stop watch from the year before. Mike would stand by my side at one stake and Calvin would be at the other. He would blow a whistle and drop a red flag. I would take off licked split. Mike would jump up and down and encourage me on. He was a great help in getting me in shape and keeping my spirit up.

After a week of steady training Calvin said, "Ms Kelly your time is faster than last year when you won the race in Monticello."

It made me so happy and important when I could please him.

As the days passed my training got more intense. Not only did I have to be in shape physically, I have to be ready mentally. That is part of winning; I had to keep focused on what I was doing.

Calvin put me on a special diet, no more treats until the race was over. This was the hardest thing to do. Treats I could easily do without, but greasy hamburgers would be hard to give up.

Jade Winds is just a few miles from the Greyhound racetrack. This is where they have the Mutt races. I couldn't believe that none of the animals in the complex had ever heard about the Mutt races.

Mike stayed with me and helped all through my training. He asked a thousand questions. He is worried about me. I explained to him, "There is no danger in the race. All the dogs that will be in the same race with me will be about my size."

As race day got near I was getting nerves, These Miami dogs have been in many more races than my competition in the

Monticello race. It was a close race in Monticello; here I will have to run faster if I want to come in first, second or third and get a trophy.

Finally the day came, Calvin and I arrived and I can hear the blowing of the bugle. The regular greyhound race is in full swing. Calvin took me to the Mutt pens. He could watch the greyhound races from where the pens were.

It's two hours before the Mutt races; all the dogs in my race are in a large pen so we could get acquainted with our competition. There is always a big mouth bragging about winning. In this race there are two of them, two long legged Chihuahua brothers. I heard that last year one of them name James came in first and Jack the other came in second. They were walking around with their chest all stuck out.

Jack said, "None of you little squirts have a chance in outrunning us. We'll come in first and second again. This year I get to come in first and James will follow me for second place. The rest of you mutts can fight over third place."

They both had a big laugh about their dull joke. I still remember what, Molly, a nice greyhound told me last year. "Don't let the ones that are bragging rattle you. That is why they are bragging and harassing to get you upset and nervous. The main thing to remember is stay calm and pace yourself."

As the time to race was drawing near I kept telling myself, "Don't get nervous and stay calm pace yourself. Stay calm stay calm."

We are all lined up at the starting gate; I will be coming out of the number three gate. I am getting nervous but am still repeating to myself everything I need to do.

The starting bell rang, we are off. I'm in the middle of the pack, James and Jack are in the lead, hollering, laughing at the others and wasting energy. Those guys are in for a rude awaking.

Around the first turn I eased up slowly and took over the lead of the pack. James looked back at me and said, "Look Jack Ms Kelly is trying for third place."

Jack said, "Ms Kelly you will not hold out, girls are just not fast enough or strong enough to win, you will be lucky to have enough energy to finish the race. You might as well quit now." They both got a big laugh out of another one of their dull jokes.

Going around the last turn I kicked it in high gear, and said to myself, "It's time to show those two goons what a girl can do."

Before they realized what was happening I was between them and running even with them. They looked at me with a shocked look on their faces. They couldn't believe that I had caught up with them so fast. I could see they had begun to tire.

Coming up to the finish line I'm a nose ahead of them. The line is just five feet in front of me when suddenly——— they moved in and squeezed me between them. Each one of them bumped me and I missed a step and they shot out in front of me and across the finish line a step ahead of me.

I was steaming mad as the announcer said, "And number three, Ms. Kelly takes third place."

I know they bumped me on purpose, they were slick and I don't think anyone noticed what they did. I ran to Calvin and tried to let him know they cheated.

It was apparent that Calvin knew what they had done and I could see that he was fighting mad, he asked another handler to watch out for me and he ran to the racing office.

I was so mad I couldn't sit still, I kept walking around in circles, this is not right I hope Calvin can do something about it.

Calvin was gone only a couple minutes when it was announced over the loudspeakers. "Everyone hold your tickets there has been a protest over the results of the race. It will take a few minutes for the judges to look at the video tape and make their official decision.

The results of first, second and third place was taken off the lighted display board.

It was deadly quiet——everyone was watching the display board and holding their racing tickets tight in their hand.

Calvin came out and was watching with me. I was so nervous I couldn't stand still. I laid down and shut my eyes, my way of blocking everything out.

Each minute seemed like hours as everyone was waiting impatiently.

All at once there was a roar from the crowd, by the time I got my eyes open Calvin was jumping for joy. I looked at the display board and number three was in first place. The judges had declared me the winner.

The announcer came on and said; "James and Jack have been disqualified for a bumping violation."

Again I was in the winner circle with Calvin, everyone was standing and applauding as the President of the race track handed Calvin the first place trophy and a check for a thousand dollars.

When we returned to our condo all the animals had already heard the news and were out by the lake waiting on me.

Mike was the first one to congratulate me with a lick in the face. I had to stay out and talk to everybody before they would let me go in the house.

I went to bed early and was asleep by the time my head hit the pillow.

THREE

MY WEDDING

It's a nice warn spring day in Miami, John and Dorothy came to visit Calvin. They were talking again about Mike and me getting married. John said, "I will officiate and we can hold it out by the lake."

"Ok I know Ms Kelly is ready so set it up." Calvin replied.

Mike and I invited to our wedding, all the dogs, cats, ducks and a pair of wild geese that had stopped in Jade Winds. This is going to be a big event.

Mike and I became very popular among the animals, especially since I had won the Mutt race.

Our wedding was still a month away, all the animals were so anxious for the ceremony they were having a hard time waiting.

John and Dorothy are having fun planning the big event. They sent invitations to every resident that had pets.

I had made friends with most of the large dogs. I was worried about them, if they came to the ceremony; there was a chance that someone who didn't like dogs would spot them and have them removed. The ones I talked to about the problem did not worry about it. One told me that if the association or anyone tried to make him leave his master could stop it. He said that a majority of the residents didn't like the rule of no big dogs allowed and if push came to shove they would vote the present members off the board and replace them with residents that owned pets.

A notice was posted in every building in Jade Winds. It read, "No dogs are allowed in Jade Winds without the approval of the board of directors." Now it's questionable whether I'm living here legally.

The day for the marriage finally came and the bank of the lake was full of people and animals. There are near a hundred balloons floating in the air, all with messages of good luck or congratulations on them. This was to be a great event and I could see that it was bringing the animal loving residents together.

I had a special appointment with my hair stylist the day before this great event. She fixed my hair up fancy and painted my nails a bright red. Calvin gave me a red collar with jewelry imbedded in the full length of it. I felt and looked like a Queen.

When Mike saw me he was so proud. He walked by my side with his chest all stuck out and prancing as he walked. We spent an hour just walking through the crowd and trying to see and speak to everyone. There was so many I know we missed a lot of them.

The pet owners were having a great time watching all their pets, as they ran every which way playing. All the pet owners came to where Mike and I are sitting and talked to us and patted us on the head. They had no idea that we knew everything they were saying. Most of them would say about the same thing, "What a cute couple, you both look great, have a happy life."

Soon we all lined up for the ceremony. We marched up to where John was standing with an open book. We could here the people clapping loudly and giving their approval as we stood in front of John.

It was a wonderful ceremony; I was nervous and glad when it was over.

After the ceremony the party began. The people had spiked punch to drink and all the animals had sweet water to drink and all the good food that they wanted to eat.

The party had just got under way when suddenly———two Dade County dog pound trucks came flying up to Calvin's condo and men jumped out with nets to catch illegal animals. The association had called them to pickup all the illegal dogs.

Everything was in array as animals started running and the people ran to stop the dog catchers. The pet owners were hollering at the dog catchers to leave. The President of the Association was telling them to be sure and catch all the large dogs first.

The dog catchers began their hunt. But by they time they got through the crowd of animal lovers the dogs had long leads on them.

Mike and I was having fun watching the action, the big dogs knew all the bushes and tunnels to escape from the dog catchers.

After an hour of trying to catch the dogs, they had only caught ten and those are older dogs that couldn't run fast.

They put the old dogs in one of the trucks and went after more. They left the trucks unguarded. A couple of the pet owners brought out a lock cutter, sneaked up to the truck that the old dogs were in, cut the lock and released the dogs. They herded the released dog into a near by pet owner's condo to hide them from the dog catchers and the President of the Home Owners Association.

After a couple hours of chasing dogs all over the complex the dog catchers had to leave empty handed. As they got in their trucks to leave all the pet owners walked along with them as the trucks slowly headed for the exit gate. The owners were clapping and laughing at the dog catchers.

The next day there was a meeting of pet owners in our condo. It was decided that all pet owners would secretly try to unseat the president. They ask Calvin if he would accept the president's position if they could elect enough pet lovers on the board to vote him in. "Calvin said, "Sure, besides this problem with outlawed pets there are problems of not enough parking places and some residents have more than the two automobiles that are allowed."

It had been three months since my marriage and fiasco with the president and dog catchers.

Calvin had completely forgotten about running for the President of the Association until late one night———there was a soft knock on the door. When Calvin opened the door it was one of the large dog's owners. Before he came in he looked all around and over his shoulder, making sure no one saw him coming into Calvin's condo.

Calvin invited him to sit down at the dinning room table. He said "I had to come at night and make sure no one was following me. I have good news; I think we will have enough members to run for the board to get you elected as President." He continued, "It would help if you know anyone in your building that would run and vote for you."

"Yes I can get Linda to run and I know there are enough residents that she knows that she would not have any problems winning." Calvin replied.

It was the 18th of February and the day for the voting for board members. The residents that were elected to the board would be the ones at their first meeting to elect the new president.

Calvin and Linda were elected from our building. This cleared the first hurdle to oust the sitting president.

The day after the election, Calvin and I were up visiting Linda. I heard Linda tell Calvin, "I got a phone call from President Bryan's best friend, he told me to be sure and vote for Bryan because he had heard that John was going to run and no one wanted John to be president." They both laughed about the phone call. Calvin said, "It's true no one would vote for John he is a trouble maker. It sounds like we have been able to keep my intentions to run a secret from his people."

I heard Calvin talking to a resident, he said, "Bryan, has been in office for ten years and he has not kept up with the changes in the residents. At onetime Jade Winds was strictly for people 55 and older, five years ago that changed and anyone could buy a condo and move in. Now there are a lot of different nationalities and many children. There is not enough parking spaces and absolutely no where for children to play. The only recreation room has been closed for years and needs new equipment. This old regime has to go."

The night of the first meeting, Calvin left for the office building to attend, since it was only a couple blocks he decided to walk. He was extremely nervous and walked to calm himself down. He had his cell phone and planned to call Adrian as soon as the new president was elected.

I sat beside Adrian as we watched television waiting on Calvin's call. Adrian was nervous but tried not to show it, me I couldn't sit still I was up and down several times. The waiting was about to get to me.

Finally the phone rang, Adrian picked it up and Calvin said only two words, "I won."

Things began changing immediately in Jade Winds. First thing that was past by the board is that small dogs are now legal again. Calvin tried but because Pit Bulldogs were not allowed in Dade County he could not get a blanket acceptance of large dogs. Each large dog had to be inspected to make sure they were not a Pit Bulldog before they would be approved to live in Jade Winds.

Calvin and his Vice President, Jean, immediately began creating new guest parking spaces. In less than a month there was over a hundred new spaces.

Residents who anticipated an overnight guest had to get a special pass by 4pm or the guest would have to pay a five dollar parking fee. This was put into effect because a lot of young people would come in late at night to party and were not guest of homeowners. Flyers were mailed out to all residents for the up coming charges for over night visitors.

A week before the charges for parking was put in effect, Calvin and I would walk around ever night seeking out cars that didn't belong to residents. Calvin would write down their license numbers. This was fun we would stay out until after midnight working the parking lots.

The first night of the required charges for overnight guest Calvin and I was out at 10: pm the time that guest had to have a pass or pay the parking fee. This was loads of fun and excitement. Calvin had requested two tow trucks be brought to the compound. He and I walked around and spotted the illegal parked cars and directed the tow trucks to them. This was something new for me to watch the tow trucks hooking up to the cars and haul them away.

The next day when Calvin returned from the association's office he told Adrian that twenty two cars had been towed. He said, "Surprising I did not get any angry residents from all the towing. I had two people that had been towed come to me and thank me for all my work and told me it was their fault that their cars got towed."

I was not getting to be with Calvin as much as I was before he was elected president. He was always at his office working on problems. I heard him tell Adrian, "This has turned into more than a full time job, after Jean and I are able to get all the immediate problems solved, things will slow down and my position with the association will not take us as much of my time as it does now. I don't mind all the work I am enjoying it"

Our door bell was always ringing, children would come and ask Calvin, "where can we ride our bikes and can we play on the grass? Condo owners came when they would have a problem concerning the common grounds, but most of them came to just talk and thank Calvin for straightening out the parking problems and for adding more than a hundred new parking spaces.

Mike and I have been together for six months. He comes and stays with me a week then we go to his master's condo and spend the following week.

I am having a great life in Miami, but I still miss our old home in Tallahassee, the dirt lane and all my good friends there.

It was early spring and I was in the kitchen as Calvin was cooking. He put a slice of fish on to fry and all at once the smell got to me and I got sick. I ran to the back door and Calvin let me out. I couldn't help it I threw up. Calvin came outside and picked me up. He had a strange expression on his face as he said, "What is wrong with you." He started rubbing my belly then he said, "I believe I know what your problem is."

He didn't tell me what he thought my problem was and this made me worry about what it could be.

Four

Birth of My Babies

The next morning I was sick again. Just smelling the eggs cooking caused me to run for the back door. When Calvin let me out I threw up again.

Adrian came out where I was and Calvin said to him, "I'm sure Ms Kelly is going to have puppies. I called the vet yesterday and she has an appointment at 2: pm this afternoon.

That solves the question of what is wrong with me. Mike is at his house and I couldn't wait to tell him he was going to be a daddy.

I am so excited, I can't wait until Calvin takes me to the vet to confirm if I am going to have puppies or not. I've been thinking about having my own puppies for a long time, I will be very disappointed if the vet tells me I'm not to have puppies.

By the time we arrived at the vet's office I was a nervous wreck. I was taken in immediately to the vet's examination room. I was in a fog as he did one test after the other. I kept looking at the vet's face to see if I could get any kind of reading on what he was thinking.

An attendant came in the examination room and took me back out to the waiting room and handed me to Calvin. She said to Calvin, "It will be about an hour before the doctor will have all the results back."

An hour! I just couldn't wait that long. Here I go again so nervous I can't sit still. I get up, lie down, walk around, jump in Calvin's lap then walk around and around in a circle going nowhere. I keep looking at the clock as the hands slowly move. The clock's minute hand made a completely circle telling me that the hour was up, but still no doctor.

Now all I could do is watch the door to his office. Finally the door knob turned and out walked the vet and headed straight for Calvin. He said, "I have good news and bad news which one do you want to hear first."

"Let me hear the good news first."

"Ms Kelly is going to have four puppies."

"What is the bad news?"

"Since Ms Kelly is so small she is going to have a hard time and might die. I am sure her puppies will have to be born by cesarean section, if you decide not to abort them."

I have never seen Calvin so tense, he sat looking out a window for a good five minutes then he asked the doctor,

"How much time do I have to make a decision?"

"I can give you a week "

"Ok I'll let you know within a week."

I was so happy I was to have four babies, but I didn't know the meaning of the words cesarean section or abort.

It was quiet at home; Calvin seemed to be in deep thought all the time.

Adrian was talking to Calvin one day and they were discussing cesarean section and abortion. Finally I found out what the definitions of the two words are. I had to someway or somehow communicate to Calvin that I want to have my puppies even if it means having an operation. I don't care what happens to me I want my babies.

I stayed right beside Calvin the whole week. I had to get him to understand that I wanted my babies.

It was the last day, Calvin had to make the decision whether my babies lived or died. He was deep in thought and I was running out of time, I had to do something. I jumped in his lap and started trying to lick his face. He looked at me and said, "Ms Kelly I wished you could make the decision about your puppies." I started whining, yelping and jumping up and licking his face. Calvin said looking at me with a surprise look on his face, "Do you understand the problem."

I yelped and jumped to his face again. He studied my face for a moment and said, "Ms Kelly I think you do understand, do you want to carry your puppy until birth?" This time I yelped louder, jumped higher and licked his face several times.

Calvin studied me for a minute or two and then said, "Ms Kelly I want to be sure, are you trying to tell me that you want to have the puppies." For the third time I yelped, jumped and licked his face. This time he said, "Well I have my answer now we will keep the puppies." I jumped for joy and licked his face again to thank him.

I still had a month to go before my babies were due. I felt good since the vet had given me medication for the morning sickness.

Mike, two Chihuahuas, Jim and Larry and I are running around together.

There are ten tall buildings, a hundred acres of open land and four heated swimming pools in Jade Winds. We are able to go all over Jade Winds, except pets are not allowed to be around the swimming pools. Too many pet owners don't pick-up after their pets.

We learned how to stay behind bushes as we traveled across and around Jade Winds to avoid humans seeing us. There are still a lot of residents that are against dogs being allowed in the compound. I know of a few cases where those dog haters caught dogs, even small ones and dumped them outside the compound.

There are a few older single homes in the compound. At onetime they belonged to the contractor, land owner, investors and some of the owner's children. They had deteriorated over the years and now were not much more than shacks. Some were occupied, the empty ones the last residents that lived there had just walked off and left their old furniture.

We loved to sneak in the empty houses and investigate what all was in them. It was fun running, playing jumping on the deserted couches and hiding in the cabinets.

Most of the empty ones were rat infested. The rats hated it when we came in to play. Jim and Larry hated rats and would try and catch them. They had made small holes in the floor to escape through. They would get under the floor where Jim and Larry couldn't get to them, laugh and make funny jokes about Chihuahuas. Jim would say, "Have your laughs one of the days I will get you.

One cold winter morning, yes, it does get cold in North Miami. A rat was in the house. He ran across the kitchen floor in front of me. Calvin didn't see him and I didn't catch him. He got behind the kitchen stove and was laughing.

I said to him, "Mr. Rat you must leave this condo immediately, neither I nor Calvin will tolerate you being in here." He said, "For get it little dumb dog, you or your master can't catch me, I will stay here until spring. I am no Mr. I am a Mrs. and I have babies coming in a few weeks. This is a nice warm house with plenty of food for me to steal so suck-it-up; I will be your uninvited guest until spring."

"Mrs. Rat I am telling you, Calvin will not allow you to stay, your kind carries fleas and disease. No matter where you hide Calvin will find you and if you don't leave I promise you he will kill you.

"Sorry little pooch, I can take care of myself he will never catch me."

A few days later I was sitting on Calvin's lap while he was watching television. Mrs. Rat ran across the floor in front of us and Calvin saw her. He called Adrian in and said, "I just saw a big rat, I'll get some poison from the store and put it out. All the food in the house will have to be kept in the refrigerator and the cabinets must be kept locked. I will take the trash to the dumpster every day so the rat will have nothing to eat but the poison."

The next day when Calvin came home from the store he had several containers of rat poison. He put some behind the kitchen stove under the living room couch, in the closets and the bedrooms.

That night after everyone was in bed and fast asleep, I got up and went in the kitchen. I could smell Mrs. Rat behind the kitchen stove, I said, "Mrs. Rat what are you doing back there."

"Your dumb master left me food back here and it's really good." She said while laughing and crunching the poison.

"He is no dumb master and you are eating rat poison." I informed her.

She immediately began spitting and gagging.

"What a mean man your master is trying to poison me!"

"I told you he would not tolerate you because of fleas and disease. Tomorrow morning when I go out to potty I will lead you over to an empty house and you can live there."

"That won't do me any good, empty houses have no food in them."

"I go over there almost everyday to play; since you are expecting babies I will bring you food."

"You know you are the nicest pooch I have ever encountered. Most every dog I have ever seen tries to kill me.

"Don't get mushy I am only doing it because you are expecting babies the same as I am.

"Oh so you are also expecting."

"Yes in about a month."

"Ok, I'll go tomorrow morning. I'll wait for you near your doggie door."

The next day I sneaked out early before breakfast, I didn't want Jim, Larry or Mike to see me escorting a rat across the compound. They would not like it and I know they would never let me live it down.

We had no more than got started when we ran in to Butch a large mean tomcat that hated rats. I saw Butch before he saw Mrs. Rat.

"Hide Mrs. Rat here comes Butch a big mean tomcat."

Mrs. Rat ran under a pile of boards.

Butch came up to me and said, "Did I see a rat walking with you?"

"If there was one it's not walking with me now."

"I will spread the word that you are palling around with rats if I find out it true."

"Not to worry Butch I would never pal around with a rat." I told him as I watch him walk away.

I was able to get Mrs. Rat to one of the empty houses without anyone else seeing me. I said, "Here we are Mrs. Rat, you better not tell anyone that I brought you here and am bringing you food."

"I won't and thanks again you are really a nice dog."

My tummy is getting a little larger, I'm just glad that I wasn't expecting to have as many as Suzie had on our old farm near Tallahassee. I can still remember her basket full of puppies and how much fun it was playing with them.

I am getting inpatient with this long waiting time for my babies to get here.

It was finally time and I was sick and feeling horrible. I'm afraid there is something wrong. I hurt all over and don't know what to do.

I'm having horrible pain and discomfort, I have to somehow alert Calvin that I need to get to the vet's office and soon. It's a good thing that he has been staying home with me instead of going to his office.

He is sitting in his easy chair, I jumped and scratched on his leg and whine. He looked down at me and said, "What wrong Ms. Kelly." I laid down in front of him and whined again. He figured out what I was trying to tell him and he jumped up and hollered at Adrian, "I am taking Ms. Kelly to the vet's office I think it's her time."

"Pam and I will come to the vet's office in a few minutes."

Calvin carried me to the car, jumped in and we headed to the vet's office at top speed. I was hoping that no policeman would catch us speeding and make us stop; I don't believe I could afford the delay.

The vet was waiting on us when Calvin rushed me in; his assistant took me from Calvin and the next thing I knew I was on an operation table.

A mask was put over my nose; I started breathing in the gas from the tank that would put me to sleep. I can only remember taking a few deep breaths.

When I woke up Calvin was standing over me. He said, Ms. Kelly you have four of the cutest Apricot babies that I have ever seen. Then the vet's assistant laid my four new babies by my side, this was the happiest moment of my life.

Five

My Children Growing Up

I had to spend the night in the vet's office under the care of a vet assistant.

The vet said to Calvin, "She is doing great but I want to keep her here overnight to make sure there are no complications. My assistant will stay with her and watch over her and the new puppies."

I had my four babies with me; I couldn't get over how beautiful they are. They all look just like my father. Their hair color is a deep dark Apricot and it's curly and wavy.

I'm so proud of my new babies, it hard to believe that all four of them are in good health and with such good color.

I would never want them to be show dogs but I am sure that they would make great ones.

Morning finally came and Calvin and Mike came to get me. Mike couldn't get over our new babies. We had three boys and one little girl. He was so proud of his new children he had to lick them and try to talk to them.

I laughed and said, "Mike you have to give them time they can't see you or hear you. You know that dogs are borne with their eyes and ears closed."

He said, "I know I'm just practicing when they will be able to see and hear what I have to say."

When we arrived home there was a large crowd of animals on the lake bank beside Calvin's condo.

Mike was the first one out of the van, he ran up to all the visiting animals and said, "Please everyone go home, Ms Kelly needs rest. I will let you know when she is able to come outside."

Some aggravated because they had waited so long and now would not be able to see the new puppies. Several were begging Mike to just have a little peek at his new family.

Mike said, "No my children will have no visitors until they get their eyes and ears open. They will be able to come outside when they are about four weeks old and then everyone can visit with them."

Calvin carried my children into the condo and I was able to walk in on my own. I'm so glad to get home.

Calvin made a small play area in his bedroom for me and my new family. It has a small wall around it so the babies can't get out. I can jump the wall when I need to go outside to potty.

I was up and about in a couple days. My first visitor was Linda from the third floor. She just had to pick up my babies and love them. I was a little worried because she was handling them so much; I let her know by scratching on her leg, whining and yelping. She finally realized I was worried and put them back in their basket. If it was anybody but her I would have growled and not let them pick them up.

Several people came to see my new family and Calvin would tell them, "Please don't pick them up they could get sick from too much handling." I was always on guard, whining, yelping and sitting at their feet, watching every move they made if anyone picked them up.

My new family is so much fun, I only leave them long enough to eat a little and rush outside to potty. I can see changes in them everyday. Each ones personality is already showing.

When they were six days old their eyes began to open and I could just make out their first word, "Mommy."

It was a warm summer day when they were four weeks old. I took them outside for the first time. It was so wonderful watching them looking and smelling everything that they came up to. The many ducks on the bank and in the lake was something that really intrigued my children; they ask me a thousand questions about them. I had to explain why there were so many colors and the difference in a wild duck and a tame duck.

The lake bank was filled with animals that had waited patiently the four weeks to see them.

Mike had to caution them not to crowd the babies. He was such a good daddy always worrying about his new family.

Calvin named my boys Sam, Dan, and Ben. My darling little girl was named Molly after the greyhound that helped me win my first Mutt race.

They were so much alike even I was having a hard time telling them apart. The only difference was that Sam's eyes were a little darker color, Dan had a joking personality and Ben was a little smaller than the other two boys. Molly was the smallest. All four had dark liquid eyes like me.

Everybody was telling me how cute they are and wooing over them. They are eating up all the popularity and complements. I know they will be spoiled rotten before they reach three months of age.

Those boys of mine are very smart they're already running around acting foolish to get the crowd to laugh. I think I have three comedians. They love to run a lot like their mother.

Sometimes I have to calm them down when they get to play fighting and one of them get hurt and a real fight starts.

Molly is quite and already a little lady. She has a strong personality and many times will put the boys in their places.

Over the next few weeks things began to settle down and I could see my boys growing each day. They learned to talk at a very early age. I decided to give them lessons in the language of ducks and geese since they will be raised around so many of them. I asked JP to lend me a hand in teaching them the duck language.

Humans think ducks just quack and there is no meaning in it, but each quack is a little different and it's easy for me to understand. Their language is really a simple language.

It wasn't long till my children were about to run me up the walls with there constant chatter, questions and arguing among themselves. Every two minutes they were asking, "Mother what is that flying or mother what is that in the lake?"

At six weeks Calvin and I took them to the vet's office for their check up and shots.

They were not happy campers when the vet brought out the needle. I had to reassure them that it wouldn't hurt much and they had to have all of their shots so they would stay healthy.

Dan said in a discussed voice, "But mother we are healthy and I don't think we need to take those shots."

"Dan this is what the shots are for, to make sure that you stay healthy," and then I remarked, "As young dogs would say, just suck-it-up and take your shots."

Dan slowly laid down rolled over on his back so the vet could give him his shots then he said, "Ok mother, just for you."

The little devil had to tell the other three that the shots hurt; he kept moaning, laid down and started crying like he was in a lot of pain. He made such a big deal out of his faking being in pain the other three headed for the exit door, desperately tried to get out. Calvin had to run to catch all three of them; they were running every which way. He finally got them all corralled and carried them back to the vet for their shots. Calvin was laughing as he said, "You little buggers thought you could get away and not take your shots, sorry but everyone has to take their shots, I don't want any sick puppies around me."

I nipped Dan on his rump for his dirty prank and told him that he had better not ever do that again.

Calvin held each one of the other three as they got their shots. They turned the tables on Dan. All of them were calling him a

36

wimp for crying over the shots. They laughed, and teased him all the way home, talking as if he meant that the shots really hurt. Dan didn't say anything to them afraid I would nip him again.

I would only let them out to potty; sometimes Calvin would watch them so I could go outside and visit with Mike and all the other animals. I loved my children but I had to get away sometimes or I would be a mental case running after those four.

My sons were growing so fast, it was no time until they were almost tall as me. Molly was growing but she was still smaller than the boys.

They are now big enough to play outside. They are very good and mind me and Calvin so well I don't worry about them.

It is time for the Mutt race again. I am over the birth of my babies and looking forward to the race.

Calvin brought the sticks out again so I could train for the coming event.

I was in good shape by the time the race was getting close. Each day I got more excited about racing. This being my third race I was not nervous anymore, but was a little concerned this time; I seemed to be a little slower. I was almost four years old and close to being passed the age for racing.

The boys were so excited about their mother being in the big race. They would spend hours watching and bragging to all the other puppies and kittens that lived in Jade Winds about their mother being in the race. All three of them walked around with their little chest sticking out and prancing like they were someone important. Molly said that she was embarrassed the way her brothers were strutting and bragging to all the puppies in Jade Winds.

I am so glad that I've been able to give my children a great start in life. I still remember what a horrible time I had growing up, until Calvin came and took me away from all my misery

As the date got closer my children would run with me while I was training. I was surprised at how fast they can run.

My children all have the beautiful Apricot color and would make great show dogs. They are really fast for their age and height; I know they would be good in Mutt racing also.

Finally the race day arrived; Calvin let my children go to the track to watch all the festivities.

My children are having a great time, running, playing and seeing new things. I'm enjoying watching them as they explored all the activities that are going on.

The Mutt race was not only a race but a festively. There are many things for people to do, watching the pig and roach races are the most popular.

There are hundreds of dogs of all different breeds, crossbreeds, large and small. People are everywhere leading or carrying their pets.

There are stands for people to buy toys for their pets, stuffed toy dogs, plastic ones that would bark and turn in circles.

My sons are having a great time watching all the people and looking at all the puppy toys.

The next thing I knew my children were begging me for a toy. Dan said, "Please mother I know that you can make Calvin understand that we want a toy."

I said, "Ok, I will try." Calvin was pulling my children in a small wagon as he walked through the stands.

As Calvin stopped and was looking at some stuffed toys, Dan started wiggling in the wagon. Calvin picked-up a squeaky rubber toy; Dan started trying to get it out of his hand. Calvin said, "You want this toy Dan?" Dan started wiggling faster and Calvin said, "Ok all four of you little squirts can have one each, they all started yipping and licking his arm, what a sight.

"See Dan it is easy to get Calvin to understand what you want." I said.

It was getting time for the Mutt race. All the dogs in my race were in an open pen to get aquatinted with each other.

Molly the Greyhound that helped me at my first race in Monticello was down here in Miami racing. I walked up to her and said, "Hi Molly."

"Ms Kelly it sure is good to see you again. Don't tell me you are going to race again."

"Sure am! I won another race since I've seen you, thanks to all your help in training me. Come with me Molly I want you to meet my four children and my master."

"Oh Ms Kelly you have children?" She asked as we walked up to where Calvin was watching my babies play.

"Oh! Ms Kelly what beautiful children you have."

All four of them had to show off for Molly.

"Molly I want you to meet your name sake, this is my daughter Molly." I exclaimed proudly.

"Ms Kelly, how sweet you named your daughter after me, I am honored, thank you so much."

Molly told me that she would give me some tips on this race, she said, "You know Ms Kelly your competition are people's pets and their masters are proud of them. They have been papered all their life. They are determined to please their masters and will use the last ounce of strength, just like you did last year. Every one of them wants to win a trophy for their master. You know Ms Kelly you are a year older and have had puppies. Your competition is young and eager to make a name for themselves."

She continued as we walked toward the racing arena, "I don't understand why Calvin entered you in this year's race."

"I know Molly but I am going to try my best."

"That is all you can do, but watch yourself and don't get hurt; you have won two races for Calvin that is more than enough. If you fall you could be seriously injured."

"I promise I will watch out and keep out of jams, I want get hurt but, thank you for caring."

As the race got closer the usual braggers were spouting out their bragging about no one would have a chance but them.

I am in number four gate this time.

A couple of young ones were nervous and scared after the two braggers got them cornered and told them, "Don't expect to win." They warned them, "If you get ahead of us we will trip you and you will fall and probably get badly hurt, just keep a little ways behind us if you want to come out of this race alive."

The trainers finally got the two nervous dogs in there gate.

One of them named John was in the gate next to me.

"Don't listen to those two braggers just run the race the best that you can." I explained to him.

The gun went off and the doors clanged open and the race is on. I'm taking my time and holding steady in the middle of the pack. Rounding the last turn I took over the lead of the pack. The two big mouth braggers are still ahead of me.

We are around the last turn and I turn on the after burners. I'm up beside of the two braggers. They look at me in surprise. I passed one of them but the other is giving me a good race.

Surprising John is coming up fast. He past the two braggers and is up even with me.

The finish line is coming up; I'm doing all I can. John is staying with me. We cross the finish line neck and neck.

It's another photo finish.

I am sitting at Calvin's feet waiting for the results, I felt so bad, I am sure I lost. But if I lose I am glad that John will be the winner instead of one of the big mouth braggers.

The scoreboard lit up, John had won. I came in second place.

Calvin bent down and patting me on the head and said, "That's OK Ms Kelly second place gets a trophy too. What you say we let your boy's race next year, it's a good time for you to retire, three races and three trophies, I don't think any dog can beat that record."

I had enough strength to jump on his leg and yelp in approval. Calvin said, "Ok you are officially retired from the Mutt races. You can help me train your sons for the next race. I know they will make good Mutt racers.

When we got back home, again there are a lot of animals sitting on the lake bank waiting for us to return. They are all congratulating me on coming in second. I thanked them and said, "That was my last race, Calvin has retired me."

"Oh Ms Kelly that is great, you can say that you retired as a big winner." They all exclaimed.

After the races the pace slowed down and everything returned to normal.

My kids are growing and learning things very fast. They had already learned the duck language very well and could understand enough of the geese and cats to hold a conversation with them.

John and Dorothy came to visit. John told Calvin that he would love to have Dan and Sam. He said, "Ms Kelly can always come over and spend time with them."

Calvin looked at all four of my children for a few minutes then said, "Five Dogs is too much for my condo. I will let you take them as soon as they are four months old, and if you promise to let them come and visit.

"I agree." John said as he grabbed Calvin's hand and shook it.

I dreaded the day that my Dan and Sam would move out. I know they will only be a couple doors down from me but it was making me sad.

At age four months Dan and Sam moved to their new home. They were excited about their home and new master.

"Don't cry mother we will see you most everyday. You know five dogs in one house are too many, this will be better for all of us," Dan explained.

My two sons, such grown-up dogs at four months, I know they will make Mike proud.

We had a going away party for Sam and Dan; they only invited their closest friends. After it was over I couldn't keep from crying as they took their rubber squeaky toys that Calvin had bought them and headed out the door to their new home.

Six

The Fighting Pit Bulldogs

I changed my routine since two of my babies had moved out. I would go out to potty after Calvin gave me my breakfast and then go visit with Sam and Dan.

Mike and I had met a couple pugs, James and Mary; they are married and have the same master.

"Ms Kelly you are lucky that you get to live with two of your children. Every time we have children they are moved to new masters usually before they are four months old." Mary commented sadly.

"Yes I am glad that Calvin let me keep two of my children. Since I had such a hard time in delivering my babies I will not be able to have anymore." I explained to Mary.

We are back playing in the old deserted houses that are still on Jade winds property. A couple more of the old homes are now deserted.

It was fun going through them and seeing what the humans had left behind.

Early one Saturday we were exploring in one of the old houses. Mike, James and Mary were upstairs. I stayed downstairs and Mrs. Rat came out from a small hole. I startled her and she started to run.

"Don't run it's Ms Kelly I won't hurt you," I said.

I was glad that I was in the deserted room by myself.

"Mrs. Rat how are you doing."

"Fine I have another litter of babies. I have finally been able to find plenty of food without going into the houses where humans live. After I met you I did go to another human's house and had a litter of babies. The humans that lived there were always drinking and having parties. My children were doing well until one night there was a party and one of my boys tried to get a drink out of the punch bowl and fell in. It scared a woman so bad she fainted and turned the punch bowl over. It was a miracle that my son was able to escape. The next day there was poison put out all over the house. I had three sick children before I could get them out of there and into one of these deserted houses."

Mrs. Rat continues, "Ms Kelly I will tell you a secret."

"What secret?"

"Now Ms Kelly you can't tell anyone, promise."

"I promise."

Mrs. Rat leaned over and whispered in my ear. "There is an old house that is in the back of the property almost covered by bushes. I get all my food in there. In the basement there is a lot of mean ugly dogs in small cages."

"Do you mean they're all locked in cages? How do they get anything to eat since no one lives there?" I asked.

"There are three guys that come in everyday to feed them. In the basement there is a room full of feed." Mrs. Rat informed me.

"Sometimes they will take some of them out and when they return they are all cutup and bleeding and hurting so bad that they are crying because they're in so much pain." Mrs. Rat explained pitifully.

"What kind of dogs are they and how do they get cutup so bad?" I asked.

Mrs. Rat was getting aggravated with my questions and exclaimed. "Now how do you think I would know what kind of dogs they are, I'm not a dog expert! All I know is that it looks like someone mashed their noses in and they have wide chest, stocky built and look very mean. They growl at each other and trying to fight each other through their cages. They are always threatening me when I eat their food. They keep saying that one of these days they will get loose and kill me. I just laugh at them, there cages are too strong and they are too dumb to learn how to open a lock. "

I heard Mike, James and Mary coming down the stairs so I ran out of the room while Mrs. Rat was still talking. I didn't want them to see me talking to a rat.

The next day Mike, Ben and Molly were scheduled to go to the vet for a check up I was by myself outside, so I headed for the deserted houses and looked up Mrs. Rat.

"Mrs. Rat will you show me where the deserted house is with the caged dogs in the basement?" I asked.

"Sure Ms Kelly follows me. I travel through the bushes to avoid all the cats. They know that I have been living in the deserted houses and traveling from one of them to the other. They are a bunch of very dumb cats, they have a lookout that I can spot a mile away. None of them are good hunters."

"Don't worry I won't let any cat get you, I will be your lookout as we move to the other building." I promised.

When we got to the house it was empty and covered with bushes, just one little path lead to the house.

I walked around the house but could not find anyway to get inside, all the doors were locked and some nailed shut.

"Ms Kelly, come with me I know where a tunnel is that leads to the basement. It's around back of the house and a little ways from the building. It was a storm cellar at one time. There is a very small tunnel that goes from the old storm cellar into the basement. That is the way that I get in. You got to promise me that you will not tell anyone. This is where I get all my food and I don't want anybody messing up my grubstake."

"I promise." I assured Mrs. Rat.

I walked down the broken stairs to the storm cellar. It was a small concrete building with a wooden roof that was about to fall in. It smelled musty and scary. The tunnel to the basement was wooden and looked like it would cave in any minute.

I slowly crept through the dark musty and scary tunnel; if I had been any larger I could not have been able to get through it. I could see a dim light and heard dogs growling at each other before we got into the basement.

When I emerged into the basement I had the surprise of my life. There are dogs in cages on top of caged dogs.

I slowly walked down the isles between rows of cages looking at all the dogs. The light was so dim it was hard to see them. They're all Pit Bulldogs and I can see that they have been trained to fight.

I felt sorry for them; most of them didn't want to be fighting dogs. They were all cut up and had old scars that had healed.

"Little girl can you open my cage?" They would beg as I passed by their cages.

As I walked through the rows of dogs I suddenly heard one of the dogs say in a loud excited voice, "Ms Kelly is that you!"

"Who said that? Who is calling my name?" I exclaimed as I quickly looked around every which way.

"Its me Ms Kelly Big Guy from the dirt lane near Tallahassee, do you remember me?"

I finally found the cage that the voice was coming from. I couldn't believe my eyes, it was Big Guy.

"Big Guy what are you doing here I thought they had you and Samson in the County Animal Control building locked up in Tallahassee."

"A man who had a scar on his face came to the control building and said he wanted to buy Samson and me. He told them he wanted us for guard dogs."

"Scar Face that is the mean man that dognapped me a couple years ago, he was supposed to be in jail for five years, I wonder how he got out." I pondered mostly to myself.

"How did you end up here and what happened to Samson?" I asked.

"Scar face lied about why he wanted to buy us; he sold us to a couple of men who own a dog fighting ring and we have been in training to be fighters. I am in a big mess I hate to fight another dog and I am in a county that Pit Bulldogs are not allowed to be in." He exclaimed sadly.

"Where is Samson?" I asked again.

"Sampson was killed in a dog fight a month ago. It was his first fight, poor Samson didn't know how to fight in the ring and he was killed within a couple minutes after the fight started."

Big Guy continued, "You know Ms Kelly I didn't want to be a mean bulldog. When I lived on the dirt lane my master was a mean man and Samson went along with what he wanted. I had to go along with Samson if I wanted to live. I am sorry for all the trouble I caused you in Tallahassee. I am really a good dog and hate this fighting game. So far I haven't been in the fighting ring but know my time is coming. I just wish I could escape and most of the other ones in here don't want to fight either and would like to get loose. Only trouble with that is since this county don't allow Pit Bulldogs, if some of us did get loose we would probably get picked up by the county dog catcher."

My heart went out to Big Guy. I said, "Let me think about it and maybe I can come up with a plan to get you and others out."

"Thanks Ms. Kelly when I lived on the dirt lane I knew that you was the smartest dog I had ever seen."

As I was walking out of the building a brindle dog started begging me to let him out. He said, "Please Ms Kelly unlock my cage and I will do anything for you. I don't want to fight and I am due to be in the ring tomorrow. I have children that I need to get back to before someone picks them up and make fighting dogs out of them."

I felt so sorry for him I began to try and get his cage open.

Big Guy hollered at me from the other end of the row of cages, "Ms Kelly STOP! That's Duke and he is the meanest dog in here. He has killed four dogs in the ring. If you let him out he will kill you!"

Duke laughed in a sarcastic voice, "Hee, hee, hee, I almost had me a little poodle, you sure are a lucky little girl I would have had you for a snack." Then he hollered down to Big Guy, "I'll get you for that, someday I will be in the ring with you and you will be history!"

I scooted out through the tunnel before things got worse. I made a beeline for the safety of Calvin's house; I had enough excitement for one day.

After breakfast the next morning I went to Mike's house and scratched on the door. When John answered the door Mike was behind him, I said to Mike, "Can you come outside I needed to talk to you."

Mike scooted around John and we headed for the bank of the lake.

I explained to Mike about the hidden deserted house and all the Pit Bulldogs in the basement.

"Ms Kelly we can not get tangled up in that mess. One thing the operation is against the law and those dogs are tuff and mean. We wouldn't have a chance if just one of them turned against us. Besides it probably won be long until the police raid the place." Mike explained.

"I know one of them name Big Guy from the farm in Tallahassee. He hates the fighting and wants to escape before he is thrown into the ring. I know if he is put in the ring he will be killed." I explained.

"Ok Ms Kelly what is your plans," Mike said in an exasperating tone.

"I don't have all the details figured out yet. It will take a lot of planning, this is the biggest problem that I every tried to solve. I have to figure out a plan to get the police notified about the illegal dog fighting. Come with me I will show you the dogs." I requested.

We scooted through the tunnel and Mike was amassed at the sight of so many Pit Bulldogs all stacked up in cages.

My first concern was how I was to get Big Guy out of the house. He was too big to crawl through the tunnel and all the doors were locked with a bugler proof lock.

I wondered around in the basement and discovered that there are four rooms to it. One of the rooms had a large cabinet turned over on its side. I walked around the cabinet and could see that the bottom had rotted out. I walked inside of it and it was pitch dark, but very roomy.

I found Mike and said to him, "Let's go back to Calvin's condo, this place gives me the willies."

When we got back to Mikes we were enjoying Dan and Sam. Dan and Sam have such a beautiful Apricot color; I am so glad that their color turned out so good. Before my children were born I was so afraid that one of them might have a white body like mine.

I said to Mike, "I have no idea how we are going to get Big Guy out of that building and out of Dade County."

"Come on Ms Kelly we don't need to do anything it's not our problem." Mike begged.

"Mike I just can't leave him in there and do nothing. We need to get the place raided but just can't figure out how to do it." I explained.

"Ms Kelly you are the smartest dog I've ever met and I know you can figure something out. I know you could get Calvin to follow you over there. You could show him all the dogs and since he is President of the Home Owners Association he would be able to do something."

"The house is locked up tight and no one can get in except."–
———It hit me like a ton of bricks, I said, "Mike I think I have it

figured out, I have got to go back and speak to someone, you wait here and I will be back in a little while."

I didn't want Mike to know I was going back to talk to Mrs. Rat. I remembered her saying that every morning three men came in to feed them. I just have to find out what time they usually show up. I'm sure I can get Calvin to follow me over there and quite sure that I can lead him to the basement.

When I got back to the house Mrs. Rat was in among the dog cages eating their food.

I waited in another room until Mrs. Rat had finished eating.

Some of the dogs were so mad because she was getting some of their food. They were promising her that when they got loose they would get her. She just laughed at them and replied, "All you fighting dogs are so dumb you can't catch anybody."

"Mrs. Rat would you come in here a minute I want to talk to you."

She came bouncing in and said, "Hi Ms Kelly, what's going on."

"I need to ask you a couple questions."

"Shoot." Mrs. Rat replied.

"Mrs. Rat I need to know when the men brings all the food and what door do they use to get in the building,"

"They are here at eight sharp and they use the front door. Just on the inside of the front door is a staircase going down to the basement."

"Thanks a lot Mrs. Rat I think I have my plan all worked out."

"What plan and what worked out?" Mrs. Rat questioned.

"Just a plan to get Big Guy out of there." I didn't tell her I was going to get Calvin to shut down the illegal dog fighting operation. She wouldn't like that since it will end her food supply.

I went back into the room where all the fighting dogs were. I had to try and talk to Big Guy without others hearing me. I called him over to the front corner of his cage and whispered in his ear.

"Tomorrow morning at 7: am I will be in and get you out of your cage. In the next room is an old large kitchen cabinet lying on it side. The bottom has rotted out and you can hide inside. I'll lead Calvin down here and I know he will call the police and all the dogs will go to the animal shelter. After they are taken away I will get you out of the house and hopeful figure out a way to get you out of Dade County. We are not too far from the county line."

"Thank you, thank you Ms Kelly!" Big Guy exclaimed excitingly.

I felt bad because I had promised Mrs. Rat that I wouldn't tell anyone about the dogs. But I just couldn't stand by and watch Big Guy and many others get killed or chewed up in the fighting ring. I will have to apology when it is all over and hope she forgives me.

I was up before 6:30am the next morning and I had to jump and yelp a lot to get Calvin up. I ran to the back door to be let out. He let me out before fixing breakfast. I made a beeline to the deserted house and hurried through the tunnel.

Big Guy was up and waiting for me. I had his cage open in no time, it was a simple lock. Mrs. Rat was correct when she called them all dummies. I cannot believe that not one of then knew how to open their cage. I heard that Pit Bulldogs were bred for muscle not brains; I now believe that to be true.

When he got out of the cage all the other dogs started howling and begging me to let them out.

"Don't listen to them Ms Kelly, those two brindles on the end of my row, Tammy and Max they are my best friends and would you please get them out." Big Guy asked.

"Ok there should be plenty room in that cabinet for all of you to hide in."

I was on a time schedule, I had to hurry back home and eat breakfast quickly and somehow get Calvin to understand to follow me back over here during the time that the man comes to bring feed to the dogs.

I looked at the clock it was ten till eight, I had to get Calvin out and to follow me quickly.

I pulled on his leg and ran to the back door, he looked at me strange and said, "What do you want Ms Kelly." I had to go back and grab his pants leg again. He said, "Ok Ms Kelly I will come outside with you.

After we got outside I ran ahead of him toward the deserted house and yelped and looked back at him. He stood looking at me and scratching his head and said, "Now what do you want to do."

It was going to take me sometime to make him understand. I again returned to him and pulled on his pants leg. That usually would get him to know what I wanted. After about three times running back and forth, pulling on his pants leg he started following me.

I had to hurry now we had taken up too much time in getting started. I hurried along and kept turning and barking at Calvin so he would hurry up.

Finally we got there in time,————but nobody was there to open the door and feed the dogs. I couldn't believe it the only day that I needed someone to come and feed the dogs they are either late or not coming. I had to keep Calvin here for a while incase they were just late.

I ran around the house smelling at everything to keep Calvin interested in what I was doing. I even took him out to the cellar but he refused to go down, afraid of a cave-in. Calvin stood looking down in the cellar and said, mostly to himself, "I got to get the maintenance crew out here and fill this in before some child gets hurt playing in it."

Mrs. Rat will be mad at me if he fills that in and she can't get in the basement anymore.

The man never came and Calvin went back to the house, I don't know what I'm going to do.

I returned to the basement to see how Big Guy, Tammy and Max were doing. I crept in the cabinet and called for Big Guy.

"Here I am over here Ms Kelly"

"You all will have to stay here overnight, the guys didn't come to feed and I can't get the doors open." I explained.

"That's OK Ms Kelly we have plenty of food and water. By the way Tammy is my girlfriend."

She came out in the light and she was a cute Pit Bulldog.

"Hi Tammy, glad to meet you."

"Hi Ms Kelly I have heard nothing but great things about you. Big Guy is always praising you about how smart you are and how you know so many different languages."

"Thanks for the complement and I will try again tomorrow. I need to get home now."

I could hardly sleep; I knew it would be harder to get Calvin to go back for a second time. I could only hope that the man would come to feed at his regular time.

I got up early and began my running back and forth and pulling on Calvin's pants leg. He said, "Ms Kelly you do not want me to go to that old house again, do you?"

When he said that, I really began jumping, barking and running back and forth.

He finally said with a long sigh, "Ok Ms Kelly this will be the last time. I have no idea what interest you have in that old house."

We arrived there at eight sharp and again nobody was there. I was getting nervous and didn't know what I was going to do. I have to keep Calvin here and he is not going to want to stay. I ran around the house but Calvin didn't follow me this time.

"Come on Ms Kelly lets go back home." Calvin said with an irritated and demanding tone in his voice.

By the time I got back around the house Calvin was walking away toward his condo. He had already walked out of sight when behind me the feed men pulled up to the house. I took off after

Calvin; I just had to someway get him back. This time I put everything into it and was jumping around, growling, barking and leaping up on his leg as high as I could.

"Come on Ms Kelly leave me alone and let's go home."

I tried one more time and again put everything I could muster up in jumping and barking. Calvin looked down at me and could see the expression on my face and said, "Ok Ms Kelly lets go back, but this is absolutely the last time."

When he rounded some bushes he suddenly stopped, backed up and peeped around them. The feed men were walking in the front door with bags of feed on their shoulders.

After they got out of sight Calvin ran to the door and peeped in. I led him to the basement stairs. Calvin slowly crept down the stairs and gasped when he saw all the Pit Bulldogs in their cages. He immediately turned and whispered to me, "Come on Ms Kelly lets get out of here."

Calvin was walking so fast that I had to run to keep up with him. As soon as he got in the condo he grabbed the phone and called the Dade County Sheriff's office.

It wasn't but a few minutes when the Sheriff was knocking on our door. He asked Calvin to take him to the house.

When we got outside there were three more police cars in the parking lot. I had to run fast to get there before the police did. I ran to the cellar and crawled through the tunnel.

The men were still feeding the dogs when I got there. I waited until they were on the back row and slipped in the room where Big Guy, Tammy and Max were hiding.

I told them that there were four police cars outside and at any minute there was going to be a raid on the house. I stayed in the old cabinet with them until we heard the police coming down the stairs.

There was so much noise and excitement going on I couldn't take it all in. The Miami Animal Control showed up with several trucks. I overheard them saying it would take them all day and probably would have to finish up the next day.

"I will be back tomorrow, sorry but you all will have to spend another night here." I explained to Big Guy.

"That's OK Ms Kelly we'll be fine."

The next day I was up early and went to Mike's house and told him to come with me.

"Ms Kelly what kind of trouble have you got yourself into. You are not going to take me back to where those Pit Bulldogs are caged are you?"

"No silly the house was raided and they are taking all the Pit Bulldogs out. Come on and we will watch them."

We went through the tunnel and sat back out of sight and watch the Animal Control people taking the last few cages out. There was a television reporter there taking films of the dog fighting pens and the few cages that had not been picked up yet.

It was another hour before they were all gone. I called Big Guy, he and the other two came out so happy they could hardly stand still.

I said you still have to be quiet, remember you all are illegal in this county and you could still be picked-up.

Mike and I took them out of the complex by crawling through a hole in the fence. When we got to a large street I told them. "You stay on this street it is only a couple miles to the county line. When you get across the line you could still be picked-up, but in that county they would try to find some one to adopt you."

I bid them fair well and Mike and I headed home. The first thing Mike said to me after we went back through the fence into the complex was, "Ms Kelly how did you know about that hole in the fence and how many times have you been out on the streets of Miami? You know it is very dangerous on the streets especially for a little dog."

I didn't want to explain to Mike and didn't want to promise him that I wouldn't go out of the complex again so I said. "I know Mike."

I was exhausted from all the activities of the last couple days. I crawled upon my pillow and was fast asleep in less than a minute.

The next morning I was up early and Mike came through the doggie door.

"Ms Kelly you got to stop taking chances like that. Those dogs are not worth you getting hurt."

"Mike something like that only happens once in a dog's life, I am sure that I will not be taking chances like that again. I just couldn't leave Big Guy in there where he would have a sure death as soon as he was put in a fighting ring.

SEVEN

DOGNAPPED

When the news about the raid on the illegal fighting dog ring was released in Jade Winds everybody was talking about it. Residents were coming to our door everyday to thank Calvin for catching the illegal dog fighting ring.

He told them, "Thanks but it was my dog Ms Kelly that should be praised she led me to the basement where the dogs and fighting ring was. Most of them didn't believe that I had led Calvin to the dogs, they would say, "That little thing, you must be kidding."

After all the excitement about the fighting Pit Bulldogs was over, I got bored, my children are almost grown and I have nothing to do.

I overheard Calvin talking to Adrian, he was going to visit his mother and brothers in Poplar Bluff, Missouri, and Adrian was going with him.

I started jumping all over his lap; I would love to go. "No Ms Kelly we have to fly to Memphis Tennessee and you can't go, dogs are not allowed in an airplane." Calvin explained.

What a bummer, I lowered my head and slinked off letting Calvin know I was not happy about the fact that I couldn't go.

I was dreading this trip to Missouri, I enjoyed staying with Donna but it will be for over a week and I know I will be bored before the week is over, I am not liking this situation at all!

The day before he was to leave Calvin was on the phone talking to Donna about boarding me. I could only catch part of the conversation. I heard Calvin say, "Oh I'm sorry you can't keep Ms Kelly I don't want to board her anywhere else, but I will have too, I am flying to Memphis and can not take her."

There was a long pause, then Calvin said, "Oh really I didn't know that. That solved the problem."

Now what did that mean, where was Calvin taking me to be boarded, I am not liking this, having to stay in a strange place, probably in a cage with a lot of strange smelly dogs, just like I had to do when we first moved to Miami. I am helpless there is nothing I can do to improve my situation.

Adrian came home from work and Calvin said, "Guess what?"

"What?" Adrian asked.

"Donna told me that we could take Ms Kelly with us. She will have to stay in a small cage during the flight. I can carry her on the plane in the cage and keep the cage under the seat in front of me."

I am so excited I can't sit still; I began jumping and yelping loud! Calvin started laughing and said to Adrian, "Would you believe her, the way she is acting and looking at me, this little girl knew exactly what we are talking about." Adrian looked at me as he started laughing, and said, "You know I believe your right."

I was so excited, I didn't care if I was in a small cage this was the thrill of my life, flying in an airplane, "WOW!"

I was on pins and needles waiting————finally the day arrived. I'm jumping around so nervous while Calvin and Adrian are packing and putting in a soft blanket in my new cage for me.

I couldn't sit still all the way to Ft. Lauderdale airport. I had to stay in my cage as we walked through the terminal to get the tickets then to the loading platform.

It seemed forever before the announcer broadcasted that our plane was loading.

The flight started off smooth and thrilling. As soon as we were in the air Calvin pick-up my cage and sit it on his lap so I could see out the window. What a wonderful time I'm having.

Coming in to Memphis things turned awful we were in a bad thunder storm. The pilot announced that we would have to circle the city until the storm passed.

The flight was getting scary; I could tell that Calvin and Adrian were worried about our situation. The wind and rain was horrible so we kept circling the airport for most of thirty minutes, and then the pilot said he was taking us in.

As the airplane got lower it began to shake and sway, I could tell that Calvin and Adrian were getting extremely worried and alarmed about the movement and shaking of the airplane.

It keeps getting worst and I am so scared I shut my eyes and put my paws over my ears.

I could vaguely hear a squealing sound and then a hard bump; I yelped, cried out loudly anticipation a lot of pain! I just knew we were crashing!

Then Calvin and Adrian both let out a loud sigh in relief. The squealing and bump were the tires hitting the runway, we were safe.

I was so glad to get out of that plane and in the rented car that Calvin had picked up to drive us the rest of the way to Poplar Bluff.

We still had three hours of driving; this is much better I can sit in Calvin's lap and see everything that is going by outside.

This land was much different than Florida. I heard Calvin telling Adrian that the white stuff growing in the fields was cotton and the tall skinny plants that looked like extra tall weeds was field corn. He told Adrian that when he was growing up the residents of all the small towns like the one he grew up in made their living working in the cotton and corn fields. Looking at those fields I'm sure it was hard work. I wonder if the people took their pets with them when they worked in the fields. I guess I'll never get that question answered.

We stopped in Poplar Bluff, Missouri and Calvin sneaked me in to his niece, Barber Jean's steak house.

After we had a lunch of steak, we were back traveling in the car; our next stop was in Calvin's home town of Qulin, Missouri fifteen miles from Poplar Bluff.

Calvin took Adrian and me around and showed us the three different houses he had lived in when he was a child and the school he attended from first grade through the twelfth.

This is a very small but nice town; I wish I had lived with Calvin when he was a little boy.

After cruising around Qulin we stopped at a small café and had lunch. Calvin called it a greasy spoon and it was the only restaurant in town

As we were leaving Qulin I kept looking back at it until it was out of sight. I would probably never see it again.

Our next stop was in Puxico, Missouri. That is where Calvin's Mother lives. She lives in a mobile home on his oldest brother Bill's big farm.

This is a large cattle farm and I am having fun following Calvin, Adrian and Bill through the cow pasture.

I am staying as close as I can get to Calvin, these large cows are giving me dirty looks and they act like they are ready to charge me. I have never been around cattle. I liked all the animals that was on Calvin's little farm in Tallahassee much better. They were all nice and friendly.

Too soon our visit with Calvin's mother, niece and brother ended and we were on our drive back to Memphis, Tennessee.

This time the flight was smooth all the way, no bumps or storms. I had a wonderful time on the trip and had a thousand things to tell the other animals in Jade Winds.

When I got back in Jade Winds all the animals had one question after another to ask, about the flight, our visit to Missouri and our flight back.

This was a big ego trip for me; none of the other animals in Jade Winds had ever flown in an airplane and had no idea where Qulin, Missouri was.

After living in Jade Winds for three years, Adrian was ready to retire. He and Calvin were talking about selling the condo. They both liked it out west and I overheard them talking about moving out there.

Adrian was not too enthused in moving since Pam would stay in Miami and go to college.

Its spring and Adrian is off work for the summer, he is a college professor. Calvin and Adrian decided to go out west for the summer. Since Pam was out of school for the summer she was included in the trip

Calvin wanted to visit his daughter in San Diego and he also had a summer home in Bisbee, Arizona, up high on a mountainside.

Since they are going for all summer and had to have a car out there, it was decided to drive out west.

Wonderful news for me, since they were driving I would for sure get to go. It was hard waiting on the trip this was going to be the adventure of my life.

The trip took three days; we had to stop a lot of times for me to potty. When we stopped for the night Calvin had to slip me into the motel rooms. All of them had signs posted, "No Pets Allowed." We didn't have any problems; no one checked the rooms for pets.

When we got to Nevada Calvin by-passed Las Vegas and headed south.

We stopped in a small town called Searchlight. At first I couldn't understand why Calvin had stopped here, then I understood when I heard him and Adrian talking, both of them had decided to move to Nevada when Adrian retired and they could sell the condo. They had decided to look for places to buy while we are out here.

I was happy and sad. I was happy to be moving out west, I had already fallen in love with the desert. I was sad because they would probably not be living in the same house.

They looked around Searchlight but found nothing that either one wanted.

We headed on down highway 95 going south. Just before we got to the turn off going to Laughlin, Nevada Adrian spotted a housing development and said, "Let's go see what they have."

"Those houses would be too much money." Calvin replied.

Adrian was driving and he turned the van into the housing development anyway. We stopped in front of a house that was called a model.

We got out of the van and Calvin carried me into the model.

I was looking out the window at several rabbits that were playing in the yard and was not listing to the conversation. Suddenly I heard both Calvin and Adrian saying at the same time, "We'll take it."

It seemed that the double garage had been turned into an office and the model is for sale. With the extra room where the garage was the house could be turned into a duplex, completely separated except the kitchen would have to be shared.

"Wow," in a twinkling of an eye we had a new home.

We traveled on to Laughlin, Nevada and crossed the Colorado River into Bullhead City, Arizona. It took about an hour for Calvin and Adrian to sign the papers for the new house.

After getting the mortgage signed we headed on to San Diego to see Kathryn, Calvin's daughter.

I had a lot of fun at Kathryn's she had a Chihuahua named Ms Bailey. There was a big fenced in the backyard and a doggie door. I had loads of fun with Ms Bailey and the visit with Kathryn.

We spent five days at Kathryn's then traveled to Bisbee, Arizona to Calvin's summer home.

The house was on a mountain side and going to the edge of the backyard I could look down on the old historical downtown of Bisbee. It was scary and I didn't get too close to the edge.

The backyard was small; I stayed in the house most of the time.

Pam and Adrian loved the place and had a great time.

I ventured out in the backyard. It was nice and large.

There were a lot of birds in the backyard. I could understand a little of what they were saying. They're a little afraid of me since I was a stranger. I tried to put them at ease by telling them I was friendly.

There are lots of hummingbirds. Calvin put out a feeder for them and they were fighting over it. I sat for hours watching them argue over the feeder.

A day before we are to leave, I went bouncing out in the backyard. I'm near a large rose bush, there are weeds that have grown up around it when suddenly———I heard a rattling sound. I instantly knew what the sound was and where it was coming from. It was a rattlesnake and he was in the bushes in front of me. I threw my breaks on and slowly backed up. My experience at the little farm in Tallahassee taught me how to deal with rattlesnakes. You just get as far away from them as you can. I stayed in the house the rest of the time we were in Bisbee.

After a stay of five days we came down from the mountain and headed back to Miami.

The trip back was much like the trip out west, three days and me sneaking in the motel rooms at night.

It would still be nine months before we were to move out west.

Calvin was still the President of the Home Owners Association in Jade Winds which kept him busy, and Adrian was scheduled to work the next school year including a short summer semester.

We settled down for another eleven months of living in Jade Winds.

It is only a couple more months before the next Mutt race at the Ft. Lauderdale race track.

Calvin had brought out the sticks to make a training area. This year I will be helping coach my two sons Sam and Dan in the art of winning a race.

Dan and Sam both wanted to participate in the upcoming Mutt race. I kept giving them all the points that Molly had given me when I was racing. Calvin put them on a strict diet and everyday they were in training and loving it. They enjoyed running as much as I do. Everyday I could tell that they were running faster and could last longer.

The only problem was they were boasting too much. All the animals in Jade Wind would come to watch them in training. This built up their ego way too much. They began boasting that they were sure to win the race. Dan said we will come in first and second, no one can beat us. I talked and talked to them about being too sure of themselves but it just went in one ear and out the other. I told them about the braggers when I was racing and how they would use up all their energy and end up loosing, but they just didn't seem to listing.

A month after Dan and Sam began their training it was time for the race.

It was a repeat of last year's race. It was a big event with a lot of booths selling everything from food to all kinds of animal toys. All my family got to go. Mike and I were walking around with our four children. We are so proud of them; they never gave us any trouble and have turned out to be good honest dogs.

Sam and Dan are in the large open pen with all the other dogs in their weight class. They are on their own, I can't help them anymore and everything is out of my paws now.

I was watching from outside the fence, my boys were strutting and bragging. I am afraid that they did not listing to me about wasting energy. I can't believe it they are jumping around and acting silly and telling all the other dogs that they don't have a chance against them. I'm afraid they are going to get embarrassed.

At least they got good starting gates, one and two.

The bell rings and they are off. My sons rush to the lead, just the opposite of what I told them to do. I just can't watch it I know exactly what is going to happen.

I shut my eyes but Ben kept telling me what was happening. At first he was all excited and said, "Mother Sam and Dan are way out in the lead. There is no dog even close to them."

"Yes Ben but the race is a long ways from being over." I explained keeping my eyes closed.

"Mother they are going around the last turn and I see a Silver Poodle catching up with them."

"I knew it; their bragging is going to make them lose." I explained to Ben still keeping my eyes shut.

"No mom the Silver Poodle is dropping back they are still in the lead. It looks like they are going to win."

I opened my eyes to look just as a spotted mix breed young dog was moving up fast. I shut my eyes again.

"Oh mom the mix breed dog has caught up with Dan and Sam. Now there are two more about to catch up. Sam and Dan are slowing down. Oh mom they have lost. All the dogs crossed the finish line ahead of them, they came in last."

Sam and Dan came slowly walking up to me with their heads down low. I felt sorry for them but maybe this will be a good lesson for them.

Dan with his head still down said, "Mother you were right we blew the race. I promise I will listen next time."

"That's OK son experience is a good teacher. I know you have learned a good lesson and will do better next time."

All the animals were happy that I would be here for another year, especially Sam and Dan since they will not be going out west with us when we move.

The next day Mike came through my doggie door and was so pumped up it took him a minute to be able to talk.

"Ms Kelly Dan has been dognapped." He declared in a shaky voice.

"Calm down and tell me what happened."

"Sam said that they were out playing in one of the old houses and a man grabbed Dan and took off."

"Let's go talk with Sam." I requested.

Sam was still crying and having a hard time talking.

"Calm down Sam and tell me what happened so we will know where to look for Dan."

"We were playing in one of the old houses and two young men grabbed Dan." Sam exclaimed.

"I thought you told me it was one man that snatched Dan." Mike exclaimed.

"No it was two young ones."

"Were they boys or men?" I asked.

"They were big but I believe they were boys."

"Well that helps a lot; they probably are still in Jade Winds." They probably think they have a new pet. We can get all the animals to watch out for them and help us rescue Dan." I explained.

I hope Calvin can help us find him.

John and Dorothy were banging on Calvin's door. He let them in. John was so frustrated his face was beet red.

"Calvin Dan is missing. We have walked all over the complex several times calling him but he is no where to be found. What else can we do?"

Calvin was stunned and didn't answer for a minute or two.

"That's awful, do you think he is lost or someone snatched him?"

I jumped on Calvin's leg and began yelping.

"What is it Ms Kelly is Dan Lost?"

I laid down and didn't move.

"Was he dognapped Ms Kelly?"

I jumped in his lap and began yelping.

"John it looks like he has been dognapped. I am sure that Ms Kelly knows."

"Ms Kelly was dognapped when we lived in Tallahassee. A gang had collected a lot of little dogs. It was everyday that somewhere in Tallahassee a dog came up missing. That is how we knew that Ms Kelly had been dognapped when she came up missing.

Since no one else has lost a dog in Jade Winds it's probably someone in the complex that seen him running loose and decided they need a dog. John did you have a collar on Dan or have a tattoo in his ear to identify him?"

"No I had not got around to it yet. I was waiting for his next vet appointment to get his shots and tattooed at the same time."

"John can you get me a picture of Dan. I will have the roaming guard to watch out for him. That will be a good start."

It has been a week and we have not found Dan. He could have been taken from Jade Winds. I have been grieving for my son ever since he disappeared. I just can't accept that he is gone. I keep remembering all the happy times that I had while he was growing up

I'm having a hard time over my loss of Dan. I do nothing but lie in my bed or sit under a shade tree on the bank of the lake remembering my Dan.

It has now been two week since my Dan disappeared. I am still in mourning over the loss of my son.

Jim and Larry came up to where I was lying on the lake bank. There was a large red dog with extra long ears with them. Larry said, "Hi Ms Kelly I want you to meet a new member of our family. This is Red, he is a registered Bloodhound."

"Bloodhound I have never heard of that breed. By the way my best friend on the little farm near Tallahassee was named Red and he was a big dog like you. What do you do Red?" I asked.

"It's good to meet you Ms Kelly, Larry and Jim have told me a lot of good things about you. My job, until I retired was on the Florida State Police Force. My job was finding lost or kidnapped children."

"How were you able to find lost children?"

"Ms Kelly my breed has an extra sensitive nose. I would be given an article of clothes that the child had worn and I could trace him down by smell. I could identify the child from a long ways just by his scent."

"That is interesting"————I said as I pondered to myself. Then an idea hit me. "Red do you think if I gave you a blanket to smell of a dog could you trace him down."

"If he is in the complex I am sure I can find him."

"Great!" I hollered "Follow me!"

I ran as fast as I could to Mike's condo and scratched on the door. John let me in and I told Mike, "Bring Dan's sleeping blanket outside for a minute."

"Ms Kelly what are you getting into now." Mike said in an irritated voice.

"Just do as I ask and come outside."

"Ok Ms Kelly I'll be there in a minute."

As Mike came out the door with the blanket, he said. "Fill me in on what we are going to do."

"Mike this is Red he is a Bloodhound and he can find anything by smell. All he has to do is get Dan's scent from his blanket and if he is in this complex he will find him."

"You mean he can find anything just by the smell."

"Yes, with just the smell, isn't that something?"

Red got a good smell of the blanket and then he said, "The scent is very weak this is going be hard to do but I am willing to give it a try."

"Great Red just do the best you can." I encouraged him.

68

We began our tour of each building and each floor. This was going to take a long time. We will probably run into some residents that will not like us climbing stairs and sniffing at each door.

It has been over a week since Red picked up Dan's scent and that was only a couple times out in an open field.

Two more weeks have passed and we haven't found him. He is just not anywhere in Jade Winds.

A month has past I'm sure I will never see my Dan again.

Six weeks have gone by since Dan was dognapped. We have all given up ever finding him. Red, Jim, Larry and I are playing in one of the old houses. As we walked across the complex going back to the lake, Red stopped in mid stride, lifted his head up high and began sniffing the air.

"I have a strong scent of Dan!" He exclaimed excitingly.

"Where at Red?" I exclaimed excitedly!

"In that car going around the corner, when it passed us I got the strong scent of Dan."

We all took off licked split toward where the car turned. By the time we got around the corner the car was out of site.

We started walking around the complex looking for the car. I know we had made at least four trips all over the complex with no more scent. We had given up and were heading home when a car passed us and Red shouted, "That's the car!"

This time we followed the car until it parked in front of a building. It was all the way across the complex from Calvin's condo.

Red was able to identify the exact condo. He said that the scent was very strong.

"How are we going to get him out?" Mike asks.

"The same way we got Big Guy out of that cage and old house." I explained.

We hurried back home and I started my yelping and jumping on Calvin. By now he knows that I want him to follow me. I ran back and forth to the door and he said. "OK Ms Kelly what have you gotten yourself into now."

We looked like a marching parade as we crossed the common grounds of Jade Winds. I was in the lead, then Calvin, Mike, Jim, Larry and Red was following in a single file.

I ran up to the door and began yelping and scratching on it. The owner opened the door and I could see Dan peeking out between the guys legs. I hollered, "Come on Dan run for it!" When he saw me he came running full speed between the man's legs. The man snapped his legs closed and almost trapped Dan.

The owner said, "What is going on here, why are you trying to get my boy's dog."

"It's not your boy's dog, that is one of my dog's pups and it belongs to John and Dorothy." Calvin informed him.

"No it's not, my boys said that a neighbor gave him to them."

"Bring your boys out here now." Calvin ordered.

While the man went in after his boys Calvin called for the security officer. By the time the man was able to get his boy outside the security officer was there.

"Where did you get this dog?" Calvin asked them.

They both were shaking but replied. "A neighbor gave him to us."

"I'm going to ask you one more time and you better not lie this time, I have worked with children a lot in my life and I know when a child is lying to me. Now one more time, tell me where you got this dog." Calvin said sternly.

They started shaking again and finally admitted that they had caught the dog on the common grounds.

"Ok I am going to let you off with a warning. If I have anymore trouble out of either one of you your father will have to move. I will not tolerate anyone stealing, especially a pet."

Oh! I am so happy I couldn't stop licking Dan's face.

He had lost some weight. He only had dry bland food to eat and the boys would not let him go potty until after dark. They kept him on a leash. The dirty old collar they had on him was too small and had worn the hair off and cut into his neck. My poor baby the pain he must have endured while he was imprisoned.

Dan said that they had taken him with them when they went on a month vacation up north. He said they made him stay in the car by himself while they stayed in motels and he got so cold he could hardly sleep. The whole trip he had very little food and water.

That was why Red couldn't find him he was way up north.

The first thing John did was take Dan to the vet. My poor baby had to be wormed and get all his shots plus an antibiotic shot for the cuts on his neck. They had not taken care of him at all; just drug him around by the neck. Some times I wish Calvin would have done more than just give them a lecture.

Eight

Lost in Tennessee

It has been a week since Dan was rescued; everything is back to our daily routine. Calvin and Adrian are planning on a trip up north to Boston where Adrian was raised and attended college. I whined and yelped until Calvin said I could go with them. Ben and Molly will stay with John and Dorothy while we are gone.

I am so excited about the trip. It's almost as many miles as driving to Laughlin, Nevada.

I need this trip after all the time I was mourning over Dan. I was sure I would never see him again. It was a miracle that Red the Bloodhound moved to Jade winds and was able to find Dan.

The big day is here, the van is all packed and I have a nice comfortable pillow between Adrian the driver and Calvin the passenger. I know this is going to be a long drive. I'm getting accustom to the long trips and am ready to hit the road anytime.

Our first stop will be in Bristol, Tennessee to visit Calvin's brother John. He is a couple years older than Calvin and has retired from driving an over-the-road truck.

John has a mobile home on ten acres, plenty of room to play. John's dog, named Jim is a large mixed breed. He is very nice and by the end of the first day we had became friends.

We are to stay here for a week; with the huge yard I know I am going to have a lot of fun.

Jim introduced me to a neighbor dog. His name is Henry and he is a Black and Tan hunting dog.

Early morning of our second day at John's, house Henry came over and asked us. "Come and go hunting with me. I will show you how to catch a rabbit and maybe we can find a raccoon. The raccoons sleep during the day but I know how to find their sleeping places."

"I'm not supposed to go beyond John's yard." I replied

"Ms Kelly I promise that we will not go any further than the edge of the woods. I will make sure I have John's house in sight at all times." Henry promised.

I thought it over a few minutes and decided to go, even though it was against my better judgment. Something keeps tells me I shouldn't go, but I didn't want to be a party pooper.

It turned out to be lot of fun. We ran a few rabbits not to catch them but to watch them run. Henry found a couple raccoons hiding in hollow limb. He disturbed their sleep and sent them climbing to the top of the tree.

"Stupid dogs they can't climb trees, why are they bothering us. Why don't you dumb dogs leave us alone!" One of the raccoons hollered down to us.

I knew enough of their language to understand what they were saying.

"We are not dumb dogs," I replied.

"I can't believe my ears, little white dog you understand our language?"

"I'm talking to you aren't I?"

"Will you take your two big buddies and leave us to our sleeping."

"Ok I'll get them to play elsewhere."

"Thanks, you're a jewel little white dog." They responded in a sarcastic tone.

I talked Henry into leaving the raccoons and hunt for other animals.

We walked a little further into the woods; Henry was trying to get the scent of rabbits or other animals besides raccoons.

"I smell an animal that we need to leave alone. It is a Bob Cat and they are mean and tough." Henry warned.

He had no more than got the warning out of his mouth when I was hit by a horrible blow from the cat and went fling through the air. I was lucky I fell into some tall grass which slowed my fall to the hard ground. The fall didn't hurt much but the cat had clawed me badly when he hit me.

The cat turned and attacks Henry and Jim. It was a horrible fight. They both were getting clawed badly. I couldn't watch the fight, I shut my eyes. I was probably more scared than I had ever been. If they lost the fight the cat might come back after me.

The fight seemed to go on for ever. The cat was screaming and the dogs were barking and yelping. The fighting moved away from where I fell and I could no longer see what was happening in the fight.

Suddenly——it got deathly quiet. I was afraid to look as something was crawling toward me. I kept my eyes closed not knowing what it was.

"Ms Kelly are you still alive?"

I opened my eyes and it was Henry. He was all cut up and bleeding bad.

"Yes I am alive but I don't think I can walk."

"Me neither and Jim is cut up bad. The good news is we were able to wound the cat bad enough that he limped off. He won't be back."

"Sorry Ms Kelly it looks like we got you in a big mess." None of us are able to walk home. We will have to stay here tonight and hope by tomorrow one of us will be able to walk out and get help." Jim said.

Looks like we are really in a jam, it's going to be awful dangerous to spend the night out here. If no body finds us we may not get out if this situation alive.

I watched the sun go down over the trees. I was so scared I didn't think I could sleep.

About two in the morning I dozed off. Suddenly I heard Calvin calling my name what seemed like a long ways off. I was hurting so bad I couldn't even bark.

Morning came and I could here Calvin still looking for me, but the hunting party was still a long ways from us. Jim and Henry are worse off than me. I don't know if they are alive or dead, I could not hear them breathing. I don't think they are going to make it.

It's getting dark again and we are still in the woods. I still can't walk or bark and I have heard nothing out of Jim and Henry. I'm hoping that they are still alive. I can still hear people hunting for us. A couple times they were close but as hard as I tried I just could make any sound. The cat's attack got to my vocal cords

Its morning of our third day and we are still lost. I'm in so much pain I can't think, I'm very thirsty and hungry. . I don't think we are going to make it. This forest is so big the ones that or looking have went on deeper in the forest thinking that we are just lost.

Suddenly,———I hear the sound of a dog howling. The sound is the same as the Bloodhound that we used to find Dan. The sound was coming toward us————Suddenly the dog burst through the bushes. He was on a leash and was dragging Calvin through the bushes.

When Calvin saw me he turned the leash loose and came running. Behind him were John and other neighbors that had been looking for us for the last two days.

I didn't remember anything else until I woke up in a vet's office. I had a lot of long gashes on my side from the claws of the Bob Cat. After getting sewed up and a pain shot I was feeling much better.

Jim and Henry were in the same room with me. They were torn up much more than I was. They saved my life but almost lost theirs by fighting the cat.

When we got back to John's house I overheard Calvin telling John. "I remembered when Ms Kelly had lost one of her sons to a couple boys who had stolen him. She had a Bloodhound friend that found him. That is where I got the idea to use a Bloodhound.

The rest of our stay at John's I kept in the house recuperation from my wounds.

Back on the road again our next stop will be Adrian's sister in Boston Mass.

This traveling cross country is getting to be great fun and I am learning a lot on every trip.

We stopped at a rest stop for me to potty. When Calvin opened the door a blast of cold air hit me. I have never been this cold before. I don't know if I am going to like it up north.

I woke up from a nap. We are in Boston, Mass and there is white stuff coming out of the sky. Calvin called it snow. Everywhere we go I learn something new.

When we arrived at Joan's house, Adrian's sister, the ground was covered with snow. I wanted Calvin to carry me but he sat me down in the snow. Its cold and I was high stepping through it. Calvin and Adrian are laughing at me.

"Here Ms Kelly try a little bit of snow," Calvin said as he put a handful in his mouth.

I took a small taste. "Wow! It's good, cold, but good.

Five minutes in the snow I was ready to get in Joan's house and warm up.

I mostly stay in the house for the rest of our visit.

Our next stop was Providence, Rhode Island. This seemed to be a nice quiet place. Adrian said when he was younger it was a wild place. I don't know what he means. Is it wild animals he is talking about? I asked myself.

Next we drove up into Maine for a Maine lobster dinner. Calvin gave me a bite of his and it was delicious, almost as good as a greasy hamburger.

Our next stop was back to Joan's house.

It was decided that we would leave for Miami at 11: PM. This was to make it past New York City and Washington D.C. before the rush hour the next morning. It worked great and we cleared both areas before morning. I was glad we were on our way home. I had enough excitement to last me for a long time.

NINE

CHRISTMAS IN NEVADA

I only got to relax at home a couple weeks. It was decided we would drive back out west during the Christmas and New Year holidays and take a van load of stuff to leave at the new home.

The day before we were to leave I supervised Calvin loading up the van. Every inch of space was used. Only enough space for Calvin and Adrian in the front seat and a pillow between them for me to sit on. Calvin built my pillow up enough so I could see outside while sitting on my pillow;

Calvin got me up before day break to feed me breakfast and go out to potty. We were on the road by daybreak. It was decided we would spend the night in Tallahassee, my old stomping ground. Douglas Calvin's son still lives there. He is a deputy sheriff for Leon County.

They all went to an Italian restaurant. Since dogs are not allowed in any restaurants in Florida I had to stay at Doug's house.

The next morning we had to wait until the van's brakes were fixed. We didn't get out of Tallahassee until about noon.

The rest of the trip was like the last one. Every night Calvin would sneak me into the motel room. I would keep quiet as a mouse so the manager would not know I was there.

We spent one night in San Antonio, Texas. Calvin's took us downtown for a river walk and a boat ride. Then we took a tour of the Alamo. This was great fun and broke up the long trip.

The third day we arrived in Palm Gardens, Nevada. I was looking forward to checking everything out. Every one was worn out from the long trip. We all were in bed by 9: pm.

I got up early for my first day in Palm Gardens. After breakfast Calvin let me out in the backyard. The yard was all fenced in with a block wall. Gates on each side of the house leads out to the street. The gates were iron bars so no animals could get in, even rabbits.

I was looking through the gate at the street when down the street came a coyote. He sees me and came trotting up to the gate. I was not afraid because I knew he couldn't get through the gate.

"Hi little girl you're new here aren't you?" He exclaimed excitedly.

"How did you learn the dog language?" I asked.

"I was raised by Randy and Wendy; they live across the street and down three houses. They also have a dog named Binge that I was raised with. Being around dogs all my life I learned the language as a small pup. By the way my name is Ray, what is yours?

"I am Ms Kelly. You mean to tell me you were raised by humans and you will not try to eat me?"

"No Ms Kelly I was raised on good tasting dog food. It makes me gag even thinking about eating a dog. I would like to be your friend."

"Wow! I have never had a coyote for a friend. I would love to be your friend."

"Ms Kelly I believe my masters just went in your house. Why don't you go in and see if you can come out in the front yard and play with me."

"Ok wait out front and I will see if Calvin will let me out in the front yard."

"You mean you have a wild coyote for a pet." I heard Calvin ask Randy as he let me in the house.

"Yes we got him just a few days after he was born. His mother was run over by an automobile. My neighbor discovered the den and there were four of them. He gave them to different families in Palm Gardens. As far as I know all four are still living. They are a couple years old now."

I started scratching on the front door and barking so Calvin would let me out into the front yard.

"Ok Ms Kelly I think its safe enough for you to go play in the front yard."

"How did you know what she wanted?" Randy asked.

"Oh Ms Kelly and I have our own language; I can tell almost every time she barks what she is wanting. She is the smartest dog I ever had."

I scooted out the door and Ray was waiting on me.

"Come with me Ms Kelly and I will show you the town. It's very small only 33 homes. I know every animal that lives here."

"I don't know about that, I am not supposed to get out of the yard," I explained to Ray.

"It will be alright if your master calls you can hear him anywhere in Palm Gardens it only has two streets and two cross streets."

"Ok let's go, give me a tour."

Ray was correct I could hear Calvin if he called anywhere in Palm Gardens.

"One thing that all the residents like about having pet coyotes around is that it keeps the rabbits out of town." Ray explained.

"Why do humans want to keep the rabbit out of town?" I asked.

"Because they eat up their plants and dig up their lawn watering pipes and chews them up to get water. You have to remember this is the desert and water is hard to come by for wild animals. It only rains a few times a year."

Ray and I became good friends and we even ventured outside Palm Gardens into the desert.

It was Christmas morning. I walked outside and couldn't believe it———snow is falling. The tops of the surrounding mountains have beautiful snow caps on them. What a beautiful sight mountains all around us covered with snow. A neighbor was talking to Calvin and I overheard him say, "The Mountains has snow on the top of them most every winter but it's rare that the snow falls here in the desert, this is only the second time since I moved here that we had snow fall in Palm Gardens.

This was a great Christmas with the snow and I got a new squeaky toy.

Before I knew it was time to return to Miami.

On the way back we stopped again in San Antonio. It was New Years Eve. We stayed in the motel and watch the ball fall in New York. When we arrived in Tallahassee we stopped and had dinner with Douglas, visited for awhile then traveled on to Miami.

TEN

WILD CHICKENS

It was nice to get back home and bring Ben and Molly home. They ask a thousand questions about Palm Gardens. They were excited about it since in the spring we would move there to stay.

John, Dorothy and Mike stopped by.

"Calvin I hear that you are moving to Nevada." John said.

"Sure am in the near future" Calvin replied.

"Since Mike will stay with us we are planning on visiting you in the near future. In fact Dorothy and I have been planning for several years that when I retire we want to move out west. John added.

"That sounds great. Come and visit anytime." Calvin replied.

Mike and I headed outside while they were still talking.

Mike and I are getting to be great friends with James and Mary the two pugs. Since we are the only married dogs in Jade winds, we became a foursome. Our favorite place to go was to the old deserted houses.

One day James and Mary were at the vet's office for a check up and Mike was off with John. I was lonesome so I decided to go play in the old deserted houses alone. There was another one that had been deserted so I headed for it. The deserted house was much like the others. A lot of old furniture was left. I was having a ball investigating the house.

"Hi Ms Kelly"

"Who said that?" I ask while looking around ever which way.

"It Mrs. Rat, I have not seen you in a long time."

"Oh Mrs. Rat it good to see you. I hope you were not hurt when they raided the house full of Pit Bulldogs."

"No everything turned out OK. When they cleaned out the house they left a couple large bags of dog food. So I still have my grubstake."

"That's great I was afraid they would take all your food away and you would be mad at me."

"I couldn't get mad at you Ms Kelly you helped me out so much every time I got into a jam."

"I have another secret to tell you."

"What is this secret Mrs. Rat?"

"There is a new kind of bird in town."

"What do they look like?"

"Well they are about the same size of the wild ducks, they have a bill like a bird, long tail feathers, and some have sharp spikes on their legs."

"Let's see,———Mrs. Rat, what you have described sounds to me like a——— chicken."

"If you say so Ms Kelly I have never seen one before and was lost as what kind of birds they are."

"There are no wild ones; all kinds have been tamed by humans. Some resident must have brought them in illegal. Where did you see them at Mrs. Rat?"

"The same house that the dogs were kept in. At night they sleep in the attic of the house. During the day they stay in the bushes and avoid all humans. I think there are three of them, at least that all I've seen."

"Thanks Mrs. Rat I think I will hang around over there and see if I can run into them."

I headed for the old house, It was getting late in the afternoon and the chickens should be getting ready to go to their sleeping quarters in the loft.

I had no more than got inside the house when a small rooster flew up in the empty window sill. When he saw me he jumped back outside and hid under a bush. I ran out the broken door and around to the bush.

"Mr. Chicken don't hide from me I won't hurt you. In the past I had a lot of chickens that were my friends." I explained in a soothing voice.

"Little dog you can speak my language, how in the world did you learn it?"

"I lived on a small farm outside of Tallahassee, Florida and there was a whole flock of chickens on the farm and I was friends with all of them."

"You mean you will not try to eat me if I come out."

"No I have never eaten another animal or bird, my master gives me all the good dog food that I can eat."

"Ok I am coming out but I warn you if you attack me, I have long spurs and I know how to use them."

"I promise go back in the old house and I will meet you in there."

"Ok I will be sitting on the old window sill."

When I returned to the house he was there. He looked a lot like Tuff Boy the leading rooster on the farm in Tallahassee, the only difference he was much smaller.

"What is you name?" I asked.

"I don't have a name, I heard one human call me a Rooster when he was trying to catch me in Key West."

"What is Key West?"

"That is what humans call an Island a long ways from here. I lived there until a man caught me and my two hens and brought us here."

"You mean that you are wild and not owned by any human?"

"Heavens yes, I have been wild from the day I hatched. In Key West all chickens are wild."

"Amazing I thought I knew everything, but am beginning to understand that you never stop learning." I said, mostly to myself.

"Do you have a name," the rooster asked me.

"My name is Ms Kelly and since you don't have a name I'll name you Joe the Rooster and call you Joe for short if that is OK with you."

"That's fine with me."

"Joe I guess you know if humans find out you and your hens are in Jade Winds they will catch you and no telling what they would do to you. Probably have you for Sunday dinner."

"I know, that's why we stay hidden"

"But they can catch you at night while you are sleeping. You need to start changing roosting places every night."

"We do change sometimes, but that is a good idea, I'll start changing every night."

"I'll try and find out a solution to your problem. There are many animal loving humans in Jade Winds but also a few animal haters."

"Thanks Ms Kelly I need all the help I can get,"

I headed back to the condo. I sat on the lake banks searching my little brain for a solution to Joe and his hen's problems. This is really going to be hard to solve, if not impossible. If they just go out in the community somebody might adopt them. But who ever picks them up may want them for dinner. There is just no where in Miami like Key West where chickens can run wild. It's just an impossible situation.

Mike came out to where I was lying on the river bank.

"Ms Kelly you have been deep in thought, what kind of mess have you got yourself into this time?"

"Mike you are just getting to good reading my mind and actions. I have run into another problem that I can't solve."

I explained to Mike about Joe and his two hens.

"Oh! Ms Kelly you are not going to get in the middle of those chicken's problems, are you?"

"I'm not into any mess, just trying to help them out. It's not like the Pit Bulldog's problem."

I have to get the problem off my mind for a while or I will go nuts. I called Ben and Molly outside and told them they could stay outside with me for the day. They were thrilled.

"Mom will you go to Mike's house and see if Dan and Sam can come out and play with us."

"Sure come along with me."

Mike came out with Dan and Sam. My whole family was together, we played the rest of the day and everyone had a great time.

"Mom can we do this again sometime soon?"

"Sure Ben, Mike and I will make sure that we do this again on regular bases."

Our condo is up for sale. Calvin and Adrian decided it was time even though it's still over four months before we move.

Everyday Calvin was showing the condo to prospective buyers. I kept Ben and Molly out of the way. Some people would not like it if they knew there are three dogs living in the condo.

The condo sold much faster than Calvin and Adrian thought it would. We still had three months before we move to Nevada.

A neighbor name Paul was visiting. Calvin was telling him about our predicament. Since the condo sold so fast we would have to find an apartment or house to rent for three months.

"I am getting ready to go to my apartment in New York City and I will rent you my Condo." Paul offered.

"How much do you want?"

"For you $700 a month and I will pay the maintenance." Paul offered.

"We will take it" Calvin quickly replied.

After Paul left I heard Calvin telling Adrian. That is a great deal, I figured we would be looking for weeks and have to pay

over a $l, 000 per month since we only want to rent for three
months.

After the condo's sale was completed, Calvin and I moved us
using a supermarket cart. Paul's condo was in the next building
from ours only about 100 feet away.

Paul's condo is on the third floor. Calvin and I use the stairs
since I am not allowed in the elevators.

We used the stairs for a week. Calvin noticed that there are
lots of pet owners in this condo building and they were taking
their pets on the elevator. After that I got to ride in the elevator
every trip we made.

It has been two months since I met Joe the Rooster and I have
not figured out anything yet. Time is getting short and I still do
not know what to do with the chickens.

A couple days later a resident came to our condo and wanted
to talk to Calvin. He told Calvin he saw a chicken on the common
grounds. As they were talking about the chickens the guy said
that in south Miami in an area called Little Havana there are a
lot of wild chickens running loose. He continued by saying he
thought a resident had brought the chickens he saw from Little
Havana.

"So there is an area in Miami that has wild chickens." I said
to myself as I begin trying to plan a way to get Joe and his hens
moved down there.

Another month has gone by, no more sighting of the chickens
by residents. I still haven't figured out how to move the chickens.
Time is running out.

I was lying out on the lake bank by myself still trying to figure
out how to move the chickens when the wise old duck JP came
up to me.

"Hi Ms Kelly long time no see"

"Hi JP how have you been."

"Fine, Ms Kelly you seem so deep in though."

"Yes, JP I am, I have a big problem."

"Tell me and maybe I can help you."

I explained in detail the problem I was facing.

"Ms Kelly let me think about it for a day or so and I will see if I can help you with your problem."

For the next several days I tried to forget about the problem and played with my children on the lake bank. They were getting spoiled from getting my full attention everyday all day long.

It had been a couple weeks since I had talked to JP when he showed up on the lake bank.

"Ms Kelly I think I have some information that might help you in getting the chickens moved."

"What is the information JP?"

"I talked to a female rat that said she knows you and she wants you to meet her tomorrow, 8: am sharp, in the old house where the Pit Bulldogs were housed. She told me that she can help you."

"Oh Thanks JP I have been about to go nuts trying to get this problem solved. It seems when I run up against a problem I can't rest until I solve it."

The next morning I was up early, scooted out the doggie door and headed for the old house.

When I got there Mrs. Rat was waiting on me.

"Hi Mrs. Rat, JP tells me that you have some information that might help me in getting the chickens moved to Little Havana before someone catches them."

"Yes Ms Kelly I believe this will help. You know there is a Spanish restaurant just outside Jade Winds near the north wall."

"Yes I sneaked outside the north wall when I led Big Guy out of Jade Winds and saw the restaurant. What about it?"

"Well I go in the restaurant a lot looking for food. I found out that there is a guy that brings several boxes of tomatoes every Tuesday. The restaurant is his last stop. I overheard him telling the restaurant owner that he lived in Little Havana and couldn't wait to get home. He gets there about 4:30pm and leaves for home about 5: pm."

Thanks Mrs. Rat I will be there next Tuesday at 4:30pm to watch the unloading of the tomatoes.

The following Tuesday I was looking forward to 4:30pm. Mike had come over and I was trying to think of an excuse to get away from him. I hated to fib to him but I know he would be mad if he knew I was in the middle of solving a problem for the chickens.

It was close to 4: pm, I had to think of something. I decided to do what all the female humans do. "Mike I have a bad headache I am going in and lay down I'll see you tomorrow."

"Ok Ms Kelly you go rest I'll go home and play with Dan and Sam."

I feel so bad for the fib but I have got to get to that restaurant before the tomato delivery man gets there.

I arrived in plenty time and found a good hiding spot in some bushes near the unloading dock.

The tomato man was on time; he unloaded all the tomatoes in his truck and then went inside to collect his money. The truck with empty boxes thrown in the back was unguarded for a good ten minutes. I can't believe how smooth things are going.

The next day I hunted up Joe and explained the plan to him. He started jumping for joy.

"Thank you Ms Kelly the food supply is getting low here. We have gotten so hungry we have been coming out in the daytime eating grass and taking a big chance on getting caught or killed. I'll keep us hidden as much as I can until next Tuesday."

The week was dragging by, I was afraid at any minute I would here that Joe and his two hens had been caught.

Finally————Tuesday came. I scampered over to the old house where the chickens were hiding.

"Joe you and your hens ready to go."

"Yes Ms Kelly we have been ready for hours."

"Ok come on I'll be your lookout on the way to the restaurant."

We no more than got started when I spotted Butch the mean cat.

"Stay in the bushes here comes Butch a mean and ornery tomcat."

"Hi Butch what's going on."

"Ms Kelly who did I see you with this time, looked like some new kind of birds. What kind are they?"

"I'm not with any birds Butch, you must be seeing things."

"Rats and odd birds, I am going to pass the word to all the dogs that you are running around with odd balls." He warned me as he walked away.

After I got rid of Butch I hustled the chickens out of the compound and in the bushes next to the restaurant.

The delivery man was on time. Everything is working like clock work. The delivery man went in to collect his money and the chickens were able to jump up in the back of the truck and hide among the many empty boxes.

I stayed in the bushes watching until the driver got in his truck and headed for Little Havana.

I was so glad and relieved when the chickens were on their way.

Eleven

Our Move to Nevada

Things slowed down, I was so happy now I can spend more time with my children. We only have about four months left in Florida I want to spend as much time as I can with Dan and Sam.

Calvin couldn't run for president since we are moving. He explained this to the board the night of the election for President. He is staying on the board as a member until we move.

I overheard Calvin and Adrian talking about flying back out west for a week at the end of the spring semester. Adrian will have a week off before he has to start teaching his last semester, an eight week summer course.

"Since we only have eight weeks left after the spring break we can pack up all our clothes that we can and leave just enough for the eight weeks. There is a washer and dryer in the condo building we can wash clothes everyday if we need too." Calvin explained.

I had a hard time waiting until we were to fly back out to Nevada. I love flying; I love to look out the window at all the clouds that are above and below me and when we fly through them.

The day finally came. We had to leave very early in the morning. Ben and Molly were taken to John and Dorothy's a day before we were to fly out. They would get to stay with their daddy and two brothers.

We were airborne by eight o'clock. We would be in the air four and half hours, but I loved flying and didn't mind the long flight.

We gained three hours in our flight to Nevada and we arrived a little after nine o'clock in the morning.

Calvin rented a car and we were on our way to Palm Gardens.

I was so excited when we entered Palm Gardens, hoping that my coyote friend Ray would still be here.

The next morning I was out early in the front yard looking up and down the street for Ray.

A rabbit came hopping down the street towards me.

"Where do you think you are going Mr. Rabbit?"

"That is none of your business little pooch."

"I will make it my business if you come on Calvin's property."

"I will go any where I want to little pooch I can easily outrun you."

"I have a coyote friend and if Ray gets after you it will be the end, you will be history."

"You are talking about that wimpy coyote that was raised in that house down the street?"

"Yes I am."

"Well I haven't seen him for over a month; hopefully something bad happened to him, like maybe he got run over by a car."

"That is a horrible thing to say."

"No it is not, he is a horrible animal always running all the rabbits out of town. We have to have food and water; you do know we are in the middle of a desert don't you?"

"Yes I know I will try to get my master to put water out for all animals."

"How can you do that, do you speak the human language?"

"No but Calvin and I have our own language. I can usually always tell him what I need and he understands it."

"I don't believe you no animal can do that."

"Ok Mr. Rabbit if I get him to leave water out for you, will you not eat his plants or dig up his yard watering system."

"Since I am sure that you can't get him to furnish water for all animals, it's a deal, and by the way my name is Jack." He exclaimed excitedly.

"That is a funny name, Jack the Rabbit." I said teasingly.

Early the next morning I took my water bowl and carried it to the door and began barking and scratching on the door.

"Ok Ms Kelly what do you want now."

"I picked up the water bowl sit it down and scratched on the door again."

"Ms Kelly do you want me to put a water dish out in the yard." I started jumping on his leg and barking.

"Ok Ms Kelly I will keep you a bowl of water outside. When we get moved out here I will put you a little fountain in the yard for you and all other animals."

The next morning I was out waiting on the rabbit to come by. It wasn't long until he came hopping down the street.

"Little dog, I can't believe it, you got the bowl of water in your yard."

"When I move out here permanently in about eight weeks, my master will put a water fountain in the front yard for animals and birds and by the way my name is Ms Kelly"

"OH! It prissy Msss Kelly," Jack teases in retaliation.

"Ok Ms Kelly I will leave all your plants alone and ask all the other rabbits that I know to do the same."

"Have you seen or heard anything about my friend Ray the coyote?"

"No and again I hope he never comes back."

"OK Jack we got off on the wrong foot by teasing each other about our names. Is there any way we can be friends."

"Sure Ms Kelly I'll sign a peace agreement with you and I'll make sure all the rabbits in this area knows that you are a friend and helper."

"That sounds great to me. We should be able to live in peace and help each other."

I looked all over Palm Gardens and even walked a little ways from the resident area looking and calling for Ray. I was beginning to believe that something had happened to him. Since Palm Gardens and the surrounding desert area is near U.S. highway 95 a lot of wild animals are killed on the highway.

I looked and looked the whole week we spent in Palm Gardens. I was still looking everywhere as we loaded up and headed back to Las Vegas to catch our plane back to Miami. I am so worried about Ray.

It was good to get back to my children; I still call them my babies even though they are all grown.

I decided that I would stay close to home for the remaining two months we had in Miami, mostly playing with Mike and our children.

It was time for another Mutt Race. We will be long gone to Nevada before the race is to be run. Calvin told John it was up to him if he wanted Dan and Sam to participate in the race.

John was excited about the boys racing again. Calvin explained to him how the boy needs lot of training and they must be put on a strict diet.

I sat my boys down and preached to them about their bragging. I explained again that was the reason that they had lost the last race.

"Mom we learned our lesson there will be no more bragging from either one of us. We want to win the race for you, dad and John."

Calvin and I sat on the sidelines and watch my boys as they trained for the race. They had grown up a lot since they lost the last race. I could tell they were sincere in their determination to do a much better job this time.

Before we knew it moving day was upon us. I supervised Calvin loading the van. It was loaded to the hilt, only enough room for Ben, Molly and me between Calvin and Adrian. Again boxes were placed under us that put us high as Calvin. My two children and I have a bird eye view of everything all the way to Nevada.

It was the night before our big move. We all went to Linda to tell her good-by. After visiting Linda for a long time we walked around and Calvin was telling everybody good-by

We were up early the next morning. All Calvin and Adrian had to do was get dressed since everything was loaded up in the van.

We loaded up and headed out of Jade winds. Before we got to the gate Calvin remembered that they had left the cell phone in the rented condo. He had pushed the door key under the door and had no way to get back in. He had to go to the office and contact the guard and have him open the door for him. So back to our rented condo we went.

Calvin and Adrian were having a big laugh about leaving the cell phone. We started our trip for the second time. As we passed the guard house and gates leaving Jade winds, I begin remembering all my adventures that I had here and began wondering what adventures I will encounter in Palm Gardens, Nevada.

COMING SOON
"ADVENTURES OF MS KELLY IN NEVADA"